THE CATHOLIC GRANDPARENTS HANDBOOK

CREATIVE WAYS TO SHOW LOVE, SHARE FAITH, AND HAVE FUN

THE CATHOLIC GRANDPARENTS HANDBOOK

CREATIVE WAYS TO SHOW LOVE, SHARE FAITH, AND HAVE FUN

LORENE HANLEY DUQUIN

Published by The Word Among Us Press
7115 Guilford Drive, Suite 100
Frederick, Maryland 21704
wau.org

22 21 20 19 18 1 2 3 4 5

ISBN: 978-1-59325-329-5
eISBN: 978-1-59325-504-6

Scripture quotations are from the Revised Standard Version of the Bible:
Catholic Edition, copyright © 1965, 1966 the Division of Christian
Education of the National Council of the Churches of Christ in the
United States of America. Used by permission. All rights reserved.

Excerpts from the English translation of the *Catechism of the Catholic
Church* for use in the United States of America, copyright © 1994,
United States Catholic Conference, Inc.—Libreria Editrice Vaticana.
Used with permission.

Pope Francis quotes are taken from the Vatican website, vatican.va.
Used with permission.

Cover design by Faceout Studios

Library of Congress Control Number: 2018930816

To my grandchildren—Colin, Ellie, Patrick, Lilia, Alaina, John, Mark, and James—
with lots of love.

Table of Contents

Introduction

What is the difference between a grandparent and a Catholic grandparent?

That's a question I've been pondering ever since Beth McNamara, my editor at Word Among Us Press, asked if I might be interested in writing a book for Catholic grandparents.

I am the Catholic grandmother of eight wonderful grandchildren, currently ranging in age from infancy through the "tween" years. I began to ask myself: *Is there something that makes me different from my friends who are not Catholic? Do I act differently? In what ways does my Catholic faith form a foundation for my relationship with my grandchildren?*

The answers to these questions unfolded for me as I started to interview other Catholic grandparents for this book. I discovered that a lot of what I did, and what other Catholic grandparents did, was not that different from what my non-Catholic friends did. Catholic grandparents live in the same secular world as other grandparents. But I began to see that Catholic grandparents tend to see that world from a slightly different perspective, one that is shaped by a faith tradition that is two thousand years old.

My interviews also uncovered some of the most painful parts of being a Catholic grandparent—especially when grandchildren are not baptized or are not being raised in the Catholic faith. Some grandparents spoke about the pain of divorce, grieving the loss of a loved one, struggles with in-laws, and other challenging family situations. These grandparents were very open and honest about the difficulties they have faced and how their Catholic faith has supported them. Some of them asked that their experiences and advice be used anonymously. I have honored those requests.

So what makes a Catholic grandparent different?

The biggest differences that I found came in areas involving prayer, family traditions, celebrating sacraments, and sharing faith. But your answers may be different from mine. For that reason, I have added questions for reflection at the end of each chapter. You may find it helpful to reflect on these questions privately, or you may want to share these questions with friends who are grandparents or with other members in a grandparent support group.

This book is intended as a guide for new grandparents, affirmation for existing grandparents, and inspiration for all Catholic grandparents. It was designed to be a handbook with short chapters on a variety of topics. Each chapter has stories, practical advice, questions for reflection, a grandparent prayer, and insights from Pope Francis. At the end of the book, there are additional ideas for sharing faith and fun with grandchildren throughout the year.

Some grandparents will sit down and read this book cover to cover. Others will read only the chapters that seem interesting or apply to their own situations. That's okay. Use this book in whatever way helps you the most.

No matter what situation you find yourself encountering as a Catholic grandparent, it is my hope and prayer that God's grace and love will surround you, protect you, inspire you, and guide you in your relationships with your grandchildren and the members of your extended family.

Lorene Hanley Duquin

—Chapter 1—

A Special Kind of Love

Several weeks before I became a grandmother for the first time, an experienced grandmother told me, "There's a special kind of love inside you that you don't even know exists until your first grandchild is born."

Her comment startled me. I knew there were different kinds of love, but I could not fathom how the love of a grandchild could differ from the love I feel for my children. It wasn't long before I found out that she was correct.

The love of a grandparent is different. It's not that I loved my new grandson more than I love my children. I love him in a different way.

- The love of a grandchild is liberating. There are no strings attached. There are no day-to-day worries about childrearing or discipline.

- The love of a grandchild is sacred. It reflects the love and generosity of God, and it instills in us a deep respect for life.

- The love of a grandchild is awe inspiring. It carries the fulfillment of past generations and the hope of future generations.

- The love of a grandchild is fun. It is a source of great joy.

The love I felt for my grandchild was, indeed, a special kind of love that I didn't even know existed. And over the years, as additional grandchildren came along, I felt an outpouring of love that expanded and deepened.

Understanding Love

As Catholic grandparents, one of the best ways to understand this special kind of love is to reflect on the ways Jesus revealed to us the depths of his love and the love of his Father in heaven. Here are some Scripture passages that can help us to better understand the love of our grandchildren from a spiritual perspective:

- **Love embraces children** (Luke 18:15-17). Jesus let the little children come to him even though some people tried to keep the children away. How do we embrace our grandchildren? How do we give them unconditional love in the same way that Jesus did?

- **Love teaches** (Matthew 13:1-53). Jesus revealed the kingdom of God by telling stories. How can we teach our grandchildren by telling stories?

- **Love is truthful** (Mark 12:14-17). Jesus always told the truth—even when he knew that people were being mean or were trying to trick him. Are we always truthful in what we say to our grandchildren?

- **Love heals** (Mark 6:53-56). Jesus always tried to help people who were sick, blind, deaf, or lame. How do we help our grandchildren when they are sick or suffering?

- **Love cares about people** (John 6:1-15). When Jesus realized people were hungry, he made sure that everyone had enough fish and bread to eat. How do we feed our grandchildren—physically, emotionally, and spiritually?

- **Love comforts** (Matthew 11:28-30). Jesus reached out to people who were sad, tired, and afraid. How do we comfort our grandchildren when they struggle with problems or difficulties?

- **Love trusts** (Luke 12:22-29). Jesus promised that when we place our trust in God, the heavenly Father will take care of us. How do we set aside any worries and fears that we might have for our grandchildren and remind ourselves that God will take care of them?

- **Love serves** (John 13:1-15). Jesus never put himself first. He washed the feet of his disciples as an example of how to serve others. In what ways do we teach our grandchildren to serve others?

- **Love forgives** (Luke 23:33-35). When Jesus was on the cross, he asked his Father to forgive the men who hurt him. How do we forgive our grandchildren when they say or do something that hurts us? How do we help them to forgive?

- **Love prays** (Luke 6:12). Jesus frequently took the time to pray to his Father in heaven. He knew that his Father's love helped guide, comfort, and strengthen him. How do we pray for our grandchildren? How do we pray with our grandchildren?

- **Love heeds the great commandment** (Matthew 22:37-39). When someone asked what the greatest commandment was, Jesus replied, "You shall love the Lord your God with all your heart, and with all your soul, and with all your mind. This is the great and first commandment. And a second is like it: You shall love your neighbor as yourself." How do we show our grandchildren our love for God, our neighbor, and ourselves?

Gifts from God

Joni Seith, a grandmother of three, says being a grandparent brings the idea of pure love to reality. "You just love them," she says, "and they come over to be loved. My five-year-old grandson was reading to me one day, and he threw himself back into me after he read the book, as if he were saying, 'Okay, now you can be proud of me and love me.'"

Teri Donner, a grandmother of seven, says the love of her grandchildren sustains her in good times and in bad times. "Sometimes when I am the lowest, one of my grandchildren will come up to me and say, 'Grandma, I love you!'" she explains. "Sometimes they'll say, 'Grandma, you make the best brownies of anyone in the whole world.' The brownies are just a mix from a box, but I tell them I make the brownies with love, and that's why they taste so good."

Diane Germain, who has six grandchildren, refers to them as "God's hugs." "My most important message to them is that I love them unconditionally, and that is what life and living are all about," she says. "God is love, and relationships built on love are the invisible thread that binds us together through time and eternity."

An Exercise in Love

If you are looking for a way to measure your capacity to love, here is a little exercise. Read St. Paul's description of love slowly: "Love is patient and kind; love is not jealous or boastful; it is not arrogant or rude. Love does not insist on its own way; it is not irritable or resentful; it does not rejoice at wrong, but rejoices in the right" (1 Corinthians 13:4-6).

Now read the passage again, but this time, replace the word "love" and all the pronouns connected to it with the word "I." "I am patient and kind; I am not jealous or boastful; I am not arrogant or rude. I do not insist on my own way; I am not irritable or resentful; I do not rejoice at wrong, but rejoice in the right."

No one is perfect in the ability to love, but this little exercise offers a goal that we can strive to achieve.

Love is always a gift of God. Wherever it is poured out, it makes its transforming presence felt.
—Pope Francis, *Amoris Laetitia*, 228

Questions for Reflection

1. How would you describe the love you feel for your grandchildren?

2. In what ways have you learned about love from the life of Jesus?

3. What are some of the things you tell your grandchildren about the real meaning of love?

Grandparent Prayer

Good and gracious God, thank you for the gift of my grand-children. Open their eyes so that they can see the depth of my love for you and for them. Fill me with your love, and allow me to become an instrument of your love to every member of my family. Amen.

—Chapter 2—

The Role of Grandparents

Crystal Crocker, who works in the Office of Evangelization and Catechesis for the Archdiocese of St. Paul and Minneapolis, stood before a large audience of older Catholics. "How many of you are grandparents?" she asked. Most of the people raised their hands.

"How many of you are not grandparents yet?" she continued. The rest of the people raised their hands.

Then Crystal asked the most important question: "How many of you are grandchildren?" The audience laughed, and all the hands went up in the air.

"We are all grandchildren," Crystal explains, "and we all know how important our grandparents were in our lives."

Dr. Karl Pillemer is a prominent gerontologist, sociologist, and professor at Cornell University who has done extensive research on intergenerational family relationships. He says, "The relationship between grandparents and their grandchildren is second in emotional importance only to the relationship between parent and child."[1]

Pope Francis frequently mentions grandparents in homilies and talks. "The words of grandparents have special value for the young," he says. "And the young know it. I still carry with me, always, in my breviary, the words my grandmother consigned to me in writing on the day of my priestly ordination. I read them often and they do me good" (General Audience, March 11, 2015).

Kim Doyle's grandmother was eighty years old by the time Kim got to know her. "She moved here [to Minnesota] from California when my aunt died," Kim explains. "She was the one who got me saying the Rosary. I could always go to visit her. I could walk there after school and get individual attention. I think of her, and it becomes clearer to me why I value what I do. She is the kind of grandma that I want to be."

The Grandparent Role

According to the American Grandparent Association, there are almost seventy million grandparents in the United States, and that number is growing, with 1.7 million new grandparents added each year. Grandparents come in all shapes and sizes, in a wide age range, with diverse educational backgrounds, and with even greater disparity in financial resources. Consequently, it should be no surprise to anyone that there is a variety of grandparent roles.

- Some grandparents are caretakers for their grandchildren, while others have no day-to-day responsibilities.
- Some grandparents provide financial assistance to their grandchildren, while others do not.
- Some grandparents are criticized for offering opinions and advice, while others are criticized for not showing enough interest in their grandchildren.
- Some grandparents have health issues that put physical restraints on their relationship with their grandchildren, while other grandparents have the energy and ability to be actively involved.

- Some grandparents are still working full-time or part-time, while other grandparents are retired.
- Some grandparents live close by, while others live far away.

Sometimes grandparents play a supporting role when a grandchild is sick or disabled. "Our oldest grandson needed occupational therapy and physical therapy," explains one grandfather. "I have taken him to weekly appointments. I have supported him with encouragement as he learned new skills. I tried to build his self-image when I detected times of doubt."

Another grandmother homeschooled her granddaughter who was having learning problems. "She liked to write," this grandmother recalls. "So I taught her how to write stories and how to keep a journal. But her favorite subject was religion. She liked learning about God and the different aspects of her faith."

Some grandparents don't have the same role with all their grandchildren. Their role may differ with grandchildren who are different ages. The roles grandparents play can also be affected by differing relationships with their adult children.

So what is the role of a grandparent?

What Grandparents Say

Marjorie Wurzelbacher has eighteen grandchildren and six great-grandchildren. She says the role of grandparents involves "loving, being loved, and having the time to really observe the uniqueness of each child."

Debbie Brown, grandmother of three, says, "Grandparents have the wisdom of experience that parents are just in the process of gaining." She sees the grandparent role as filling in the cracks.

Teri Donner, grandmother of seven grandchildren, warns that the role of grandparent is different from the role of parent. "I think you have to remember that these grandchildren are not your children. They are your children's children. I think you must be very careful about the way you offer opinions and give advice. Grandparents fill a very important role, but it is not to tell the parents what to do."

Rose Mary Buscaglia, who has ten grandchildren, acknowledges that even though you are not the parent, a grandparent can have a very powerful role. "I would tell grandparents: You are a leader in your family. You have wisdom. Part of your job is to help shed light on whatever is happening in the lives of your grandchildren."

The bottom line is that the role of a grandparent is unique to each family. One of the biggest mistakes families can make is not talking about the role of the grandparent. Successfully defining your role as a grandparent is essentially a matter of sharing your expectations, listening to the hopes that the parents express, and reaching an agreement that works for everybody. Sometimes the process will be easy. Other times it will be more challenging. Praying for inspiration and guidance is the best advice of all.

What the Experts Say

In his book *The Grandparent Guide: The Definitive Guide to Coping with the Challenges of Modern Grandparenting*, Dr. Arthur Kornhaber, a psychiatrist and founder of the Foundation for Grandparenting, identified the following roles that grandparents play in family life:

- The storyteller, who passes down family history and preserves family traditions.

- The mentor and teacher, who offers guidance and assistance in all areas of life.

- The nurturer, who provides emotional support and unconditional love.

- The role model, who demonstrates the importance of faith, morality, and personal integrity through the witness of their lives.

- The playmate, who creates an element of fun and adventure.[2]

I would like to greet all grandmothers and grandfathers, thanking them for their valuable presence in families and for the new generations.

—Pope Francis, Angelus, July 26, 2015

Questions for Reflection

1. How would you describe your role as a grandparent?

2. What factors surfaced as you discussed your role as a grandparent with your children?

3. In what ways has your role as a grandparent changed with different grandchildren?

Grandparent Prayer

Lord Jesus, guide me as to what my role should be with my grandchildren. Teach me to love as you love. Give me the strength and the courage to become the best grandparent that I can be. Amen.

—*Chapter 3*—

A Grandparent's Vocation

Several years ago, Ken and Marilyn Henry took their first trip to England. Marilyn was wandering around Westminster Cathedral in London when she saw a brochure on the table with the question "*Did you know Jesus had grandparents?*"

"My middle name is Anne," Marilyn recalls, "and I knew St. Anne was Mary's mother. But I never connected the dots that Mary's parents were Jesus' grandparents."

Marilyn turned the brochure over and started to read about the Catholic Grandparents Association, an international organization with chapters in local parishes. The association offers support and encouragement to grandparents in their vocation.

"I had never heard of this," Marilyn admits, "but I knew I needed it. We have eleven grandchildren, and I always prayed with them, but I knew I needed something like this in my life to support me as a grandparent."

Marilyn said a little prayer and took the brochure home. She ended up starting a chapter of the Catholic Grandparents Association in her parish in Houston, Texas. Today she is the contact person for the Catholic Grandparents Association in the United States.

What Is a Vocation?

A vocation is a call from God. Traditionally, the Church has identified three specific vocations: the married life, the single life, and the religious life. Most grandparents have experienced the call to married life—a vocation as a married couple. The vocation of a grandparent is an extension of the original call to the Sacrament of Marriage.

Fr. James Mallon, host of *Grandparents,* a video series for the Eternal Word Television Network (EWTN), points out that during the nuptial blessing in the Rite of Marriage, the priest prays that the couple will live to see their children's children. "It is a reference to the future role a married couple will play with their grandchildren," he explains. "What characterizes the vocation of a grandparent is a call to pray and intercede for grandchildren so that one day you may praise God with them in heaven."

Marilyn Henry describes the vocation of a grandparent as the last important vocation. "I don't like the word 'last,'" Marilyn jokes, "but it is true. Right now, at this time in our lives, being a grandparent is our vocation."

Catherine Wiley, the founder of the Catholic Grandparents Association, is passionate about promoting awareness of the vocation of grandparents, which she describes as being "rooted in love." She acknowledges that, like all great callings from God, the vocation of grandparent makes great demands.

"It is a work that calls for great sensitivity, delicacy, and thoughtfulness," she explains. "It is unobtrusive, never overbearing, and always respectful of the rights and values of others, especially of parents. It involves always being at hand when needed but never imposing oneself, never interfering; knowing when to offer a helping hand or a word of advice, but also knowing when to stand back. This is indeed a demanding program, but it is important to stress that we are doing something vital for God."

An Answered Prayer

Catherine Wiley is a native of Ireland, but she and her husband, Stewart, raised their children in Walsingham, England, a tiny village that has been a center for pilgrimages since medieval times. One day, as Catherine was praying, she wondered what she could give Our Lady for a birthday present that would delight her.

"The idea came," she recalls, "of a grandparents' pilgrimage to honor and thank Our Lady's parents, St. Joachim and St. Anne, for all they have done for us down through the ages, particularly the transmission of faith. This would truly delight her."

On Saturday, July 26, 2003, the feast of St. Joachim and St. Anne, the first annual grandparents' pilgrimage to the National Shrine of Our Lady in Walsingham took place. The pilgrimage was so well received that four years later, Catherine Wiley organized a grandparents' pilgrimage to Our Lady's Shrine in Knock, Ireland, on the second Sunday in September, which has also become an annual event.

News about the grandparent pilgrimages spread to other countries. In 2009, the Catholic Grandparents Association was officially launched. Since then, chapters of the Catholic Grandparents Association have been forming all over the world, and the group has received Vatican approval.

Prayer and Support

As part of their support for the vocation of grandparents, Marilyn Henry's chapter of the Catholic Grandparents Association in Houston begins each meeting with prayer and a count of the number of grandchildren represented. "We might be praying for 101 grandchildren," Marilyn says.

Marilyn recognizes how important it is for grandparents to learn about their faith, and so the group frequently has guest speakers. She also plans activities that include grandchildren. At one of their meetings, Marilyn's husband, Ken, who is a deacon in their parish, gave grandparents and their grandchildren a tour of the church. "The grandchildren could try on vestments and see where everything is kept," Marilyn recalls. "They will always remember that."

The chapter also encourages Catholic social action and stresses the importance of involvement in the parish. Last Christmas the group bought gifts for two needy families. Members volunteer to read stories to children while their parents are busy at the parish food bank, and they help with the children's Liturgy of the Word. They always plan something special for the feast of St. Joachim and St. Anne.

During every meeting, members share what is happening in their lives. "I hear beautiful stories of joy, but there are also stories of despair that break my heart," Marilyn admits. One of the biggest concerns is grandchildren who are not practicing their Catholic faith. The group also offers support and consolation to grandparents whose families are embroiled in divorce, custody fights, and other kinds of dysfunction.

One grandmother came to the very first meeting, but afterward she sent Marilyn an e-mail saying she could not be part of the group anymore. Nearly three years later, the woman returned. She explained to Marilyn that she had stopped coming because her daughter-in-law refused to allow her to see her grandchildren. The woman decided to say the Rosary every day for her daughter-in-law. When the daughter-in-law finally relented and allowed this grandmother to see the children once a week, she decided to come back to the group. "I think the support she received from the first meeting stuck in her mind, and she knew she needed to pray," Marilyn says.

One of the goals of the Catholic Grandparents Association is to reach more grandparents and to nurture their vocation as grandparents. Step-by-step instructions for how to start a chapter of the Catholic Grandparents Association and a suggested format for meetings can be found on the group's website, www.catholicgrandparentsassociation.org.

The Grandparents of Jesus

There is no mention of St. Joachim or St. Anne in the Bible. But according to Catholic legend, this faithful couple could not conceive a child. After years of prayer and fasting, an angel appeared to them and announced that they would have a daughter. St. Anne promised that they would dedicate this child to God. We celebrate the birthday of Mary, who was conceived without original sin, on September 8.

The Church celebrates the parents of the Virgin Mary, the grandparents of Jesus, Saints Joachim and Anne. In their home, Mary came into the world, accompanied by the extraordinary mystery of the Immaculate Conception. Mary grew up in the home of Joachim and Anne; she was surrounded by their love and faith: in their home she learned to listen to the Lord and to follow his will. Saints Joachim and Anne were part of a long chain of people who had transmitted their faith and love for God, expressed in the warmth and love of family life, down to Mary, who received the Son of God in her womb and who gave him to the world, to us. How precious is the family as the privileged place for transmitting the faith!

—Pope Francis, Angelus, July 26, 2013

Questions for Reflection

1. What did you think the first time you heard that grandparenting was a vocation?

2. How do you live your vocation as a grandparent?

3. How do you help other grandparents recognize and live their vocation?

Grandparent Prayer

Gracious and loving God, help me to recognize my vocation as a grandparent. Send your Holy Spirit to inspire me with ways to live this new vocation by passing on my Catholic faith to my grandchildren. Surround me with your love, and support me with your grace so that I can become the kind of grandparent that you want me to be. Amen.

Chapter 4

A New Baby

The birth of a new grandchild is a monumental event—especially if it is the first grandchild in the family. Kathy Powalski helped both of her daughters when they came home from the hospital with new babies, but she was very careful about what she did.

"I always let the new mother tend to the baby," she explains. "At times I held the baby, but I was not the principal caretaker."

Instead, Kathy concentrated on housework. "I made beds, cleaned up the kitchen, did laundry, got dinner started, and answered the phone."

Kathy only offered advice if she was asked. "If I didn't think they were holding the bottle right, I would try to say in a nice way that perhaps this might work better. I would never say, 'You're doing it wrong. That's not how to do it.'"

When friends or relatives came to see the baby, Kathy would go upstairs and let them have time with their visitors. "They would always ask me to stay," she recalls, "but I would tell them this was their special time with their friends. After dinner I would leave them alone again. This was their family time. They need that time to talk over the day. So I would go back upstairs and read."

If awards were given out for grandparents, Kathy would get highest honors. She respected her daughters' need to bond with their new babies. She recognized the ways she could be most helpful, and she offered her daughters valuable support without making any demands. Hers is the kind of humble, selfless role that grandparents are called to, and it is not always easy.

Being Humble

"At first my daughter-in-law wouldn't even let me hold the baby," one grandmother says. "I was so hurt. I didn't know what to do. I just kept praying for her, and I wrote her little notes apologizing for anything I might have done to hurt her. My husband said, 'I can't believe you are writing these apology letters when you haven't even done anything.'"

This grandmother sensed that if her daughter-in-law was harboring bad feelings, it might help if she apologized. "I knew that she held all the cards," the grandmother explains. "If she said no, I would never see my grandchild, so I was going to be as humble as I could be. If she wanted me to jump through hoops, I would jump through hoops, because I did not want to lose the relationship with my grandchild."

Her strategy worked. She still doesn't know the reason for her daughter-in-law's negative attitude toward her, but it doesn't matter. She sees her grandchild on a regular basis now, and the tensions have dissolved. Her daughter-in-law even signs notes, "Love you."

"It's like a whole new relationship because I turned it over to God, and I did not try to force the issue," this grandmother explains. "Now I just look at the whole thing as a blessing."

Words to the Wise

Here are some ways grandparents can inadvertently anger or upset the parents of a new baby:

- **Showing Up Unannounced**

Some grandparents are so excited about the new baby that they want to be with the baby all the time. But remember, this new family needs time alone. Don't ever show up uninvited or unannounced. If the parents want you there, they will let you know. "You have to let them bond," one grandmother explained. "I have friends who practically tried to move in with the family. It did not work out well for anybody."

- **Doing the Wrong Thing**

You might want to pick up the baby or change the baby or burp the baby, but a wise grandparent does not do that without permission. A new mom can be very possessive. It is important to show your respect for her wishes. "As excited as I am about being a new grandmother, I also try to remember when my children were born and how my mother-in-law kept interfering," one grandmother admits. "I don't ever want to be that kind of grandmother."

- **Saying the Wrong Thing**

We all want what is best for our grandchildren because we love them. But we must be careful when we express opinions that the parents of our grandchildren might find insensitive or hurtful. We may not, for instance, like the name they have chosen for their child. We may not agree with their decisions regarding the latest trends in childbirth. We may not agree with the sleeping arrangements for the baby, or how the baby will be fed, or what the baby wears. We might think the baby looks like our side of the family, but it's probably a mistake to say so. We need to remember that it's not our baby, and unless we are asked for our opinion, it is sometimes better to say nothing. When we do say the wrong thing, an immediate apology is in order. "I have friends who are so pushy that their kids don't even want them around the grandchildren," one grandmother said. "I keep telling them, 'You can't talk to your kids like that.' They say, 'Well, this is how I am.' And I say, 'Then you will have to suffer the consequences for your words.'"

- **Making Comparisons to Other Grandchildren**

You may be thinking about how alike or how different this baby is from another grandchild, but unless the parents ask, don't make comparisons. The parents don't want to hear stories about another grandchild. It only breeds unnecessary feelings of competition that can quickly lead to resentment. "It's hard sometimes, because you see these differences, and your first inclination is to point them out," one grandfather says. "But I have learned the hard way that if I want to say something, I'll say it to my wife, privately."

Understanding Temptations

Our Catholic faith assures us that temptations are very real, and they can wreak havoc in our lives. Grandparents might not think about temptations in regard to grandparenting, but they may find themselves tempted toward envy, irritability, self-pity, and negativity. Keep in mind that temptation is not a sin, but temptations can lead to sinful behaviors. It's important to recognize temptations and refuse to act on those feelings. The best protection against temptation is prayer because it invites God to come to our aid. Talking about temptations to a priest or spiritual director can also help.

> The family is the setting in which a new life is not only born but also welcomed as a gift of God.
>
> —Pope Francis, *Amoris Laetitia*, 166

Questions for Reflection

1. In what ways do you help when there is a new baby in the family?

2. What temptations have you experienced as a grandparent?

3. How has your Catholic faith helped you to become a wiser grandparent?

Grandparent Prayer

Thank you, Lord, for the gift of new life in my family. Help me to become a good grandparent. Strengthen me in the face of temptations. Dispel any feelings of competition, jealousy, or resentment that surface. Give me the courage to focus on what is best for the new baby and the other members of my family. Amen.

—Chapter 5—

How Things Have Changed!

Christina Lewis, a registered nurse and health educator, teaches ninety-minute classes for new grandparents at the Catholic Health System in Buffalo, New York. "Grandparents are experts in childraising because they raised their own children," she explains. "So I am not doing a baby-care class. I try to show the grandparents what is different today in caring for infants and why things have changed."

Most grandparents are surprised at how much things have changed, especially in regard to safety issues. These changes aren't just the latest fads or trends. They are recommendations based on solid research on safety hazards for infants. The greatest fear among health professionals like Christina is that grandparents might rely on outdated ideas that could unintentionally cause serious harm.

For example, in a recent study by Dr. Andrew Adesman, MD, nearly half of the grandparents surveyed thought that ice baths were a good way to bring down a child's high fever. But ice baths are in fact dangerous because they can cause hypothermia.[3]

This is just one example of how things have changed. If you want to know more, imagine that you are seated in a new grandparent class with Christina Lewis. Here are some of the things she would tell you:

Sleep Safety

One of the biggest changes in infant care revolves around sleep safety. The latest recommendations from the American Academy of Pediatrics is that babies should always sleep on their backs. Fear that babies lying on their backs will choke is unfounded because the structure of a baby's air passages and gag reflex will prevent that from happening. There is a much greater risk of babies suffocating while lying on their stomachs or tipping over onto their stomachs from a side position. Medical studies have proven that babies who sleep on their backs are less likely to die from Sudden Infant Death Syndrome (SIDS).

And there should be nothing in the baby's crib—no blankets, no stuffed animals, no bumper pads—because these increase the risk of suffocation or strangulation. Instead of being covered with blankets, infants are now swaddled or put into a sleep sack.

Overheating can also be a danger; cool temperatures for sleeping are essential. Premature and low-weight babies need special consideration in this regard; doctors will advise parents about how to maintain body warmth for these infants.

"The American Academy of Pediatrics also recommends that babies sleep in the same room with their parents until they are twelve months old," Christina says. "They don't want the baby sleeping in the same bed, but they want the baby in a bassinet or crib in the same room. It's because the baby's sleep cycles and breathing begin to mesh with the parents, and the parents can hear if the baby starts to gag or choke. It also transitions the baby to better nighttime sleep cycles, and it helps the parents to get more sleep as well."

Breastfeeding

"I never breastfed my children," one grandmother admitted. "I don't know anything about it!"

In her classes, Christina discusses why new moms are encouraged to breastfeed and how important it is for grandparents to be supportive. "Studies show that there are fewer hospitalizations when babies are breastfed in the first year," she notes.

Many moms, especially those in the workplace, pump their milk so that other caretakers, including grandparents, can feed the baby breast milk from a bottle. "I talk about what's changed in terms of sterilizing bottles," Christina explains. "We don't recommend sterilizing anymore because we want the babies exposed to a little bit of bacteria to reduce allergies. You can just wash the bottles in the dishwasher."

Solid Foods and Changing Diapers

"In the classes, I talk about solid foods for babies and some good ones to introduce," says Christina. "I encourage parents and grandparents to follow the advice of their pediatrician." She doesn't demonstrate how to change a diaper unless someone in the class asks, because she does not want to insult the grandparents. "Instead, I talk about differences in diaper changing today. For example, we don't recommend baby powder anymore. We use cream for diaper rashes."

Booster Shots and Car Seats

"A few weeks before my granddaughter was born, my daughter told my husband and me that we had to get whooping cough shots before we would be allowed to hold the baby," one grandmother recalled.

The Center for Disease Control and Prevention warns that grandparents, who may not even realize that they are sick, can unintentionally cause severe illness and death in infants. The Tdap vaccine protects against whooping cough, tetanus, and diphtheria. The immunization wears off over time, so even if grandparents received the vaccine as children or had the disease when they were young, they should receive a Tdap booster shot at least two weeks before seeing the new baby.

"I also encourage grandparents to get flu shots during the flu season," Christina adds.

She is especially concerned about car seats. "The leading cause of death for kids in the United States is auto accidents," Christina says. "Part of the problem is that there are more vehicles on the road, and they are traveling much faster. A properly restrained child in a car seat is more likely to survive a crash. But the reality is that nine out of ten car seats are being used incorrectly or installed incorrectly. So it is important to have your grandchild's car seat checked and to use it properly."[4]

Spoiler Alert

"When my kids were growing up, we were told not to spoil them," one grandmother admits.

Christina tells grandparents that you can't spoil a baby before six months of age. "Infants don't have the capability to manipulate," she explains. "I encourage grandparents to hold the baby as much as they want. Having as much face-to-face time and skin-to-skin time as possible is important for brain development, for language development, and for learning. We also encourage grandparents to talk to and sing to the baby."

A Positive Response

Christina Lewis estimates that 90 percent of the grandparents who come to her classes admit that their daughter or daughter-in-law insisted they attend. But at the end of the class, almost all the evaluations say, "Even though I was forced to be here, I really learned a lot, and I'm glad I came!"

How to Find a Grandparent Class

If a grandparent class sounds like something you would like to do, ask your pregnant daughter or daughter-in-law if they received any information about classes from their obstetrician or from the hospital where they will deliver. You might find that your local community education program or senior center offers grandparent classes. If there are no grandparent classes in your area, look into the possibility of starting one with the help of a childbirth educator or a registered nurse.

Jesus says of himself: "Learn from me for I am meek and lowly in heart" (Matthew 11:29). This is his spiritual portrait, and it reveals the abundance of his love. Meekness is a way of living and acting that draws us close to Jesus and to one another. It enables us to set aside everything that divides and estranges us, and to find ever new ways to advance along the path of unity.

—Pope Francis, Homily, November 1, 2016

Questions for Reflection

1. What changes have you noticed in the recommended care of babies and infants?

2. Has it been difficult for you to accept these changes?

3. In what ways do you see these changes as something positive and valuable?

Grandparent Prayer

Lord, give me the humility to admit that, even though I raised my own children, things have changed in terms of child safety. Instill in me a desire to learn. Help me to be the kind of grandparent who always seeks what is safe and what is good for my grandchildren. Amen.

Chapter 6

Babysitting

Yolanda Sosa was getting ready to retire from her job when her son and his wife, and then her daughter, announced that they were having babies. "How would you like me to babysit for you when you go back to work?" Yolanda asked.

Her son and his wife jumped at the chance. Her daughter graciously declined. "Oh, no, Mom," her daughter said. "I could never do that to you."

Yolanda was surprised. "It's kind of sad," she told her co-workers. "I offered to babysit for my daughter, and she doesn't want me to."

"Just wait until the baby comes," one of her co-workers replied. "She'll change her mind."

The babies were born less than four weeks apart, and Yolanda and her husband ended up babysitting both of them. "It was like having twins," Yolanda says. "I would put them in their car seats and feed both of them at the same time. I would put them both in the playpen, and they enjoyed each other's company. All of their milestones happened around the same time. They made their First Communion together. They were confirmed together. To this day, they are very close."

Yolanda is now babysitting her three youngest grandchildren. "We spend time with them every day, because we pick them up from school, and they stay here for a couple of hours until their mother picks them up," Yolanda explains. "I think it is wonderful to be around my grandkids. But I still hear a lot of people say, 'I'm not going to babysit my grandchildren. I already raised my kids. They can find someone else.'"

To Babysit or Not to Babysit

Most grandparents are thrilled to have the opportunity to spend time with their grandchildren. But babysitting on an occasional basis when the parents need to get away by themselves is one thing. Making a commitment to babysit on a regular basis while the parents go to work is an entirely different story.

Some grandparents who are too young to retire might be reluctant to give up their jobs or to cut back on their work hours to babysit during the daytime. Likewise, working grandparents might feel too tired to commit to babysitting on a regular basis at night. There are also grandparents who want the freedom to travel, to volunteer, to pursue hobbies, or to maintain social contacts with friends. Some grandparents may already be committed to caring for their own elderly parents who need assistance.

Health can be a factor; a grandparent might not have the energy or the physical ability to lift or carry a child safely. Distance can play a role in a grandparent's ability to babysit. Patience can be another factor; grandparents might not feel as if they can control an unruly child without getting upset.

As a basic rule of thumb, whenever you are asked to babysit— on a regular basis or occasionally—it's okay to say no. Don't feel guilty. Agreeing to babysit when you don't want to do it only leads to frustration and resentment. It's not good for you or for your grandchildren.

"The important thing is to communicate clearly your reasons for not wanting to babysit," one grandfather advises.

"Offer to help pay for the cost of child care if you are financially able. But don't get locked into doing something that you know is not going to be good for anybody."

Before You Say Yes

Chris Gill, who has fifteen grandchildren, warns that you should think carefully about the future before agreeing to babysit for your first grandchild. "Right now it might not sound like a lot to say you can babysit three days a week," she says. "But if you have more than one child, you are going to be expected to do the same for all of them. I babysat for everybody. I watched all of the kids for one or two days a week."

If You Say Yes

When you agree to babysit—whether it's for a few hours or on a regular basis—it's essential to sit down and talk about what is expected from everyone involved. Your vision of what it means to babysit may be very different from what your son or daughter envisions. Keeping the lines of communication open is critical. Asking questions, sharing ideas, and listening lay the foundation for a good experience for everyone.

Some Dos and Don'ts for Babysitting

- **Set boundaries.** Let's say you have a prior commitment to your parish prayer group, or you like to go to morning Mass. Make sure that everyone understands that these things are important for you. It may be okay in the case of an emergency for you to give these things up, but if you are frequently asked to forgo activities that are important to you, resentments might grow.

- **Respect boundaries.** Accept the parents' preferences for feeding schedules, nap times, and discipline. You may think you have a better way of doing things, but children need consistency, and it's up to the parents to decide how they want their child to be raised.

- **Talk about location.** Some grandparents prefer to babysit in their own homes. Others prefer to be at the child's house.

- **Talk about emergencies.** Know exactly what the parents want you to do in case your grandchild becomes ill. Minor accidents can be handled with bandages and kisses. But talk ahead of time about what is expected if something major happens.

- **Don't undermine the parents.** Never give your grandchildren the impression that you don't agree with a parent's way of doing things or that you would do things differently.

- **Always ask permission.** Don't ever take your grandchildren someplace without first asking the parents if it is okay.

- **Pretend it didn't happen.** You may witness the first time the baby rolls over or sits up or crawls or takes a first step, but a wise grandparent will let the parents think that they are the first ones to see these milestones.

- **Keep communicating.** If things go awry or if you think something should be changed, talk about it with the parents.

- **Have fun.** One of the best parts of babysitting is spending quality time with your grandchildren. Look for creative ways to have fun.

> Our way of asking and responding to questions, the tone we use, our timing, and any number of other factors condition how well we communicate.
> —Pope Francis, *Amoris Laetitia*, 136

Questions for Reflection

1. How do you feel about babysitting your grandchildren?

2. If you do babysit for your grandchildren, how did you reach an agreement with your son or daughter about what this would involve?

3. What are the most challenging things about babysitting a grandchild?

Grandparent Prayer

Lord, guide me as I take care of my grandchildren. Help me to be attentive to them and to recognize their needs. Give me patience and understanding. Increase my love for them. Help me to be a good grandparent. Amen.

—Chapter 7—

To Our Grandparents' House We Go!

Marjorie Wurzelbacher's house has everything that her eighteen grandchildren and six great-grandchildren could possibly want. "I have a playroom in my basement," she says. "Outdoors we have space for Frisbee, beanbag toss, and a wading pool. Nearby we have a public park with bicycle and walking trails, water play, sand, slides, and swings. A short drive away we have a zoo, amusement park, aquarium, and museums. Sometimes I give the parents the money for these things while I stay home and fix a meal for when they return."

Going to their grandparents' house is a big deal for grandchildren. When the website KidsHealth surveyed three hundred kids about vacation preferences, the responses included the Grand Canyon, Mount Rushmore, Disney World, and Grandma's house.[5]

Whether grandchildren are coming for a short visit, a sleepover, or an extended vacation with their parents, smart grandparents will prepare for their arrival. Here are some things you might want to consider:

Baby Basics

"Most of the time when they come to your house, they are going to eat, so you might want a high chair and some bibs," says Chris Gill, an experienced grandmother of fifteen. "Having a changing table will save your back. I fill mine with diapers, wipes, and baby rattles. The parents love it when they come over, because everything is right there."

If your grandchild uses a pacifier, Chris recommends having a few extras on hand. If you will be driving with your grandchild, you will need a car seat. It's nice to keep a stroller at your house for taking walks. Having your own portable play yard, which can be used as a bed or as a playpen, is a good idea. Don't resurrect an old crib from the attic or the basement; it may not be safe.

Chris suggests shopping at garage sales and consignment stores for gently used baby equipment and toys. "Some people have one baby and get rid of everything," she explains. "I've gotten beautiful things. Just make sure everything is up-to-date for safety standards."

Childproofing

As babies grow into toddlers, childproofing is extremely important. Start by putting away any heirlooms, photos, or other keepsakes that might be accidentally broken. Yes, you can teach grandchildren to respect your things, but do you really want to spend your time protecting objects when you could be having fun? Childproofing is easier.

Take a walk through your home and look for potential hazards. Unintentional poisonings cause more emergency room visits than automobile accidents. It is always better to be safe than to be sorry.

House Rules

It's okay to set up specific rules at your house. Kids actually behave better when they have boundaries that allow them to play freely within specified limits. For example, you can make Grandma's office or Grandpa's workshop off-limits. You can specify that playing the piano is okay, but pounding on the piano is not allowed. Tossing balls and running might be designated as outdoor activities.

Some grandparents have a special cupboard or drawer with toys that is always accessible to grandchildren. The other cupboards and drawers are off limits. Let older kids know ahead of time whether they can use your computer and get food from your refrigerator.

"I have some very simple rules for their behavior when they come to my house," one grandmother says. "No hitting, no fighting, no whining, no yelling. All I have to do is ask, 'What are my rules?' and the bad behavior stops instantly."

Having Fun

It's a good idea to have a supply of books, games, and basic art supplies for your grandchildren. A sleepover in the family room or a treasure hunt in the attic is always fun. The key is making sure that your grandchildren are safe—no matter what you choose to do at your house.

Checking Your House

Here are some of the most dangerous things for babies and small children in a grandparent's house:

- Cords on window blinds: children can become entangled in these and strangle.
- Freestanding televisions, bookcases, and dressers that can be pulled over: these can crush a child.

- Dishwasher or laundry soap pellets that look like candy.
- Dangerous cleaning supplies under a sink.
- Prescription and nonprescription drugs on a countertop.
- Old toy boxes with lids that crash down.
- Batteries for hearing aids, cameras, and remote controls that could be chewed or swallowed.
- Unprotected electrical outlets, in which children can poke fingers and other objects.
- Dangling cords on lamps and small appliances.
- Tablecloths that can be tugged.
- Pens, scissors, and letter openers on a desktop.
- Houseplants that can be pulled over or eaten.

Dear grandfathers and grandmothers, thank you for your example of love, dedication, and wisdom. Continue with courage to bear witness to these values! Let not your smiles and the beautiful brightness of your eyes be lacking in society! I accompany you with my prayers—and do not forget to pray for me as well.

—Pope Francis, Address, October 15, 2016

Questions for Reflection

1. How safe is your home for grandchildren? Have you walked through your house with an eye to finding and fixing potential hazards? If not, when will you do your "home inspection"?

2. What rules do you have for grandchildren when they come to visit?

3. What do your grandchildren love the most about coming to your home?

Grandparent Prayer

Gracious and loving God, help me to make my home a safe haven for my grandchildren, a place where they feel loved, a place where they can have fun, a place where they can make memories that they will cherish throughout their lives. Amen.

Chapter 8

The Other Grandparents

"**A**nother big issue that no one wants to discuss publicly is your relationship with the other grandparents," one grandmother admitted. "Being a grandparent is a tricky thing because you are working with another whole family, and the only thing you have in common is that your kids got married and had a child."

While many in-laws have found ways to peacefully coexist before and after the wedding, the birth of a first grandchild is often the trigger for feelings of competition, jealousy, and ill will between grandparents. These kinds of feelings arise for a variety of reasons:

- Some new grandparents are fearful that their grandchild will love the other grandparents more.

- Some new grandparents resent the other grandparents' financial status and their ability to offer their grandchild expensive gifts.

- Some new grandparents secretly disliked the other grandparents from the moment they met because of their personalities or the way they conduct themselves.

- Some new grandparents disagree with the other grandparents' values or the way they raised their children.

The good news is that the raw emotions new grandparents feel often subside over time, as both sets of grandparents fall into an acceptance of where they fit in their grandchild's life. One of the big factors in this acceptance is the birth of additional grandchildren. But until that happens, some new grandparents might wrestle with painful emotions.

Feeling Left Out

One of the biggest issues is when one grandparent gets more access to the grandchildren than the other grandparent. "The other grandmother is always there, always called upon," one grandparent complains. "I feel left out because she is the chosen one."

Sometimes the mother of the new grandchild feels closer to her own mother. She may go to her mother for advice or share more information with her about the baby than she shares with the paternal grandparent. "This started before my grandson was born," one grandmother confessed. "My daughter wanted me in the birthing room, and she told her mother-in-law to stay outside in the waiting room. I felt bad, but it was what my daughter wanted, and she was the one going through childbirth."

"Our son gave us our first grandchild," one grandfather said. "It was obvious from the start that my daughter-in-law's family took precedence over my wife and myself. But as the baby got older, we found our place in his life. Sometimes you just have to be patient."

While some mother-daughter relationships are strong, that is not always the case. Sometimes the new mom has a strained relationship with her mother, and she gravitates toward her mother-in-law. "I have a friend in this situation," one woman said. "She has always had issues with her daughter. I would never say this to her, but I think maybe the mother-in-law is more in tune with the daughter. She is not as judgmental or demanding. It's an interesting dynamic, but my friend still feels left out."

In families where there has been divorce and remarriage, the situation can become complicated. There can be up to eight grandparents of one child. Things can be even more difficult if the child's parents are divorced, and the custodial parent sets limits on a grandparent's visitation.

There are also situations in which a sister or a best friend can take the leading role in the life of a newborn child, and both sets of grandparents feel left out.

Avoiding Comparisons

Don't fall into the trap of comparing yourself to the other grandparents. It is important to remember that your relationship with this baby is not a competition.

"The other grandparents have a lot more money than I do," one grandmother said. "There was no way I could compete. It took me a while, but I eventually began to see that you don't need material things to show your love for a grandchild. They love it if they can sit on your lap and you can read to them, or tell stories, or recite nursery rhymes. You can take them for a walk. You can play with their toys. There are so many things you can do that don't cost anything."

Keeping Your Feelings in Check

One of the best ways to deal with negative feelings is to remember that how you feel is not as important as how you behave. Here are some helpful hints:

- It's okay to talk about your feelings to a trusted friend or adviser. But gossiping about your feelings of exclusion or making nasty remarks about the other grandparents will only make things worse—especially if they find out you are talking about them behind their backs.

- You may feel a little jealous, but don't let it show. Trust that your grandchild's love will be strong enough to embrace everyone on both sides of the family.

- Remember that you are responsible for your own sense of peace and happiness. Maybe your expectations for your relationships with your grandchildren are out of line.

- You don't have to be best friends with the other grandparents, but it is important to be kind and respectful when you are together. No one is all good or all bad. Try to find their positive attributes. Try to see the ways you complement each other in your grandchild's life.

- If you are the favored grandparent, try to be inclusive of the other grandparents.

- If you can develop a good relationship with the other grand-parents, everyone benefits—especially at holiday time if everyone can get together as one big, happy family.

"We are very good friends with the other grandparents," one grandmother says. "We get together with them a lot. But there are still times when I feel jealous—like when we are all together and our grandchildren run to them first. I try not to internalize it, but I do feel it. It's just the way it is. I try to remember that there are also times when they run to me first. You have to keep all of this in perspective."

An Attitude of Gratitude

Sometimes the best way to overcome negatives feelings is to cultivate an attitude of gratitude. For example:

- **Gratitude can be an antidote to jealousy.** When you start to compare yourself to the other grandparents, force yourself to think of all the little things about your grandchild that you are grateful for.

- **Gratitude can be an antidote to insecurity.** When you feel as if you're not as good as the other grandparents, force yourself to think about your God-given gifts and talents and the many ways you contribute to your grandchild's life and well-being.

- **Gratitude is an antidote to worry.** When you start to worry about what your grandchild might think about you in the future, force yourself to think about all the things your grandchild loves about you today.

- **Gratitude is an antidote to sadness.** When you feel down, force yourself to think about how grateful you are to be the grandparent of such an amazing child.

Cultivating an attitude of gratitude is one of the best gifts you can give to yourself and to the other members of your family. It's not difficult, but like any new skill, it takes time and determination. Keep in mind that an attitude is just a habitual way of thinking. When you cultivate an attitude of gratitude, you begin to see yourself, other people, the world around you, and the God who made you in a new and exciting way.

> Whereas love makes us rise above ourselves, envy closes us in on ourselves. True love values the other person's achievements. It does not see him or her as a threat. It frees us from the sour taste of envy. It recognizes that everyone has different gifts and a unique path in life. So it strives to discover its own road to happiness, while allowing others to find theirs.
> —Pope Francis, *Amoris Laetitia,* 95

Questions for Reflection

1. How would you describe your relationship with the other grandparents?

2. In what ways do you deal with envy and other negative emotions?

3. What things in your family make you feel grateful?

Grandparent Prayer

Lord, help me to be gracious and loving as you are gracious and loving. Teach me to be kind and merciful as you are kind and merciful. Give me the strength I need to overcome negative feelings with feelings of gratitude for all the good things you have given to me and to my family. Amen.

—*Chapter 9*—

Long-Distance Grandparents

Rich and Mary Bleyle live in New York. They have four grandchildren a thousand miles away in Georgia and three grandchildren eighty-eight hundred miles away in New Zealand. They have always been long-distance grandparents. When their grandchildren in Georgia were little, the only way to keep in contact was by telephone and snail mail. "I would send packages with toys, books, and clothes," Mary recalls. "They would send photos to us. We talked on the phone. As the kids got older, they would call Rich when they had questions about their math homework."

The Internet changed everything. By the time the Bleyles' grandchildren in New Zealand were born, the family used technology such as video chats, e-mail, and messaging streams to share photos and family news.

"My grandson in New Zealand shows me his toys on Face-Time," Mary notes. "He gets very excited about opening the packages I send, but mailing things does get expensive. I took one big package to the post office that cost $192 to mail. The clerk told me to keep coming back because I was keeping the U.S. Postal Service in business!"

The Bleyle family also plans vacations together—sometimes to the beach and sometimes to the mountains. Rich made sure his grandchildren learned how to ski.

Rich and Mary travel to Georgia for graduations, school concerts, sporting events, and other important milestones for their grandchildren. Traveling to New Zealand is more of a challenge, but they manage to get there occasionally.

Their efforts are paying off. Their grandchildren all know and love them.

Distance Doesn't Matter

In an Oxford University study, the grandchildren surveyed insisted that it did not matter how far away their grandparents lived. With the help of modern technology, grandchildren said, they could still maintain a close relationship with their grandparents.

You can't hug a grandchild during a video chat, but you can blow kisses, sing songs, read stories, and talk about what's happening in their lives and in your life. "They can see your face and hear your voice," one long-distance grandfather said. "You can show them how to draw funny pictures and teach them how to make paper airplanes."

Tackling Technology

The Archdiocese of Minneapolis and St. Paul offers technology workshops for grandparents in the computer lab at a Catholic school. Students from the school teach the grandparents how to log on and use the new technologies on the computer and on their smartphones.

"We promoted that workshop with the grandparent group in our parish," says Kim Doyle, who serves on the grandparent advisory board for the archdiocese. "These grandparents came back the next week, and they all had text messages on their phones from their grandchildren, who would text, 'I love you, Grandma' or 'I love you, Grandpa.' It was wonderful. We were all crying at these messages, and the grandparents kept saying, 'Thank you so much!'"

Making the Best of It

There are many reasons why grandparents and grandchildren end up separated by distance. Careers, climate, adventure, and a desire to be closer to the other side of the family are just some. Sometimes the grandparent moves away, and sometimes the grandchildren move.

If you were a hands-on grandparent and have recently been separated from your grandchildren, you may find yourself immersed in a grieving process with all the classic stages of shock, anger, sadness, and eventual acceptance. "I couldn't stop crying for several weeks after they left," one grandmother admitted. "Everywhere I looked, I saw reminders of my grandchildren, and I felt so sad."

The best way to get through the grieving process is to talk about it with friends or in a support group. It's okay to feel sad, but for the sake of your grandchildren, strive to be positive and optimistic when you talk with them. Acknowledge that you won't be together as much physically but that you will still be connected to them in other ways.

Making Visits Special

One of the best parts of being a long-distance grandparent is a visit with your grandchildren. When you visit, you are immersed in their lives for the entire time. Whether they come to you or you go to them, you eat meals together, go on adventures, share stories, and have fun. Take lots of pictures so that you can mail a photo book to your grandchild after the visit.

Thank God for the quality time you can spend with them. Be grateful for the opportunity to make memories that all of you will treasure.

When You're Apart

Here are some suggestions for long-distance grandparents for those times when they are away from their grandkids:

- Learn about the different options modern technology offers for staying in touch.

- Set up specific times when you can talk on the telephone or video chat.

- Think ahead of time about things you want to ask about their friends, their school, or their activities.

- Have a special song or story to share with young children.

- Pray together with your own special prayer or by asking God to bless all your family members.

- Agree to watch the same movie or television show so that you can talk about your favorite parts afterward.

- Mail interesting stories or funny cartoons from newspapers or magazines that might interest them.

- Send a package with homemade cookies, crafts, or other surprises.

- Share photos of any changes at your house—new furniture, new landscaping, a remodeled kitchen, or even the changing seasons in your backyard.

- Stay upbeat. No one wants to talk to a grump.

Technology Tips

There are plenty of technology tools available to long-distance grandparents. Some are more complicated than others. All of them require that you have a computer with Internet access, a smartphone, or a tablet device.

For keeping in touch with everyone in the family at the same time, there are a number of free group messaging apps available. For most people, the easiest method of communicating with more than one person is using a mobile device to set up a group for sharing text messages, photos, and videos.

Social media apps such as Facebook and Instagram allow you to share photos, videos, hyperlinks to news stories, recipes, and messages. The sites can be set up so that only family members can view what is shared.

For video chats, Apple users can access FaceTime. If you have an android device, you will have to use Skype or another free video call and chat app, such as Tango, which can be used with any kind of mobile phone or tablet.

Ask other grandparents what technology tools they use. Or ask your grandchildren for help. Then find the technology platform that works for you and your family members.

The real question . . . is not where our children are physically, or whom they are with at any given time, but rather where they are existentially, where they stand in terms of their convictions, goals, desires and dreams.

—Pope Francis, *Amoris Laetitia*, 261

Questions for Reflection

1. How do you maintain contact with long-distance grandchildren?

2. What is the most difficult part of being far away?

3. What are some of the things you do to make visits special?

Grandparent Prayer

Dear Lord, you know how hard it is for me to live so far away from my grandchildren. Help me maintain close relationships with them. Inspire me with creative ways to show them how important they are to me and how much I love them. Amen.

Chapter 10

Maintaining a Close Relationship

When Debbie Brown's son came to visit with his wife and their children, her son asked if they could go someplace nice for dinner. "I was on board for that," Debbie recalls. But as the day wore on, her twin grandsons were having such a good time playing that Debbie offered the option of staying at home and getting pizza. "Whatever you want to do is fine with me," Debbie said. "You are our guests!"

One of her grandsons immediately stopped what he was doing and said, "Grandma, we aren't guests! We are FAMILY!"

Debbie was elated. Her grandchildren live seven hundred miles away, and she doesn't get to see them very often. Her grandson's words proved that despite the distance, they still maintain a close family relationship.

Relationships Take Work

Whether you live close to your grandchildren or far away, good relationships don't happen automatically. Creating a strong family bond takes work.

In 2001, Vern L. Bengtson, a professor of sociology at the University of Southern California, and a group of colleagues tried to determine how close relationships among grandparents, parents, and children can be achieved in modern society. They identified the following six elements that are essential to what they call "intergenerational solidarity." These elements still apply to maintaining strong relationships today:

- **Associative Solidarity** involves the frequency of contact among family members. It can be face-to-face contact, but it doesn't have to be. Writing letters and e-mails, talking on the telephone, texting, and engaging in video calls are other ways of maintaining contact with grandchildren, whether you live two miles away or two thousand miles away.

- **Affective Solidarity** focuses on the level of emotional attachment between grandparents, parents, and grandchildren. Feelings of affection, warmth, closeness, mutual respect, trust, understanding, and love form the foundation for meaningful relationships. When there is a close relationship between the grandparents and their adult children, a close relationship with grandchildren usually follows. The strong emotional bonds formed with grandchildren when they are young tend to remain strong as the grandchildren grow older.

- **Consensual Solidarity** reflects the level of agreement among generations on family values, beliefs, and attitudes. When grandparents, parents, and grandchildren share their Catholic faith, their relationship is strengthened—especially when family members can pray, attend Mass, and get involved in parish activities as a family. When families have different faiths, they can still maintain close relationships. They just need to focus on other shared values and attitudes.

- **Functional Solidarity** involves the patterns of financial, physical, and emotional support among the generations. It reflects the degree to which family members help each other and share their time and resources with one another. This involves everything from the grandparents offering to babysit to the grandchildren helping grandparents with cutting the grass or raking leaves. There is nothing more reassuring than knowing grandparents, parents, and grandchildren are willing to step up and assist when someone in the family has a need.

• **Normative Solidarity** refers to the strength of commitment among generations in terms of performing family roles and meeting family obligations. When grandparents, parents, grandchildren, aunts, uncles, and cousins see themselves as one big extended family, with each person having a special place in the family and each person connected to the family as a whole, it strengthens the family bond.

• **Structural Solidarity** involves the closeness maintained by the family because they create opportunities for family interaction. Family vacations and gathering together for holidays, birthdays, anniversaries, and celebrations of sacramental milestones are important in cementing relationships.[6]

Think about your own family in relation to these six elements. Ask yourself how you, as a grandparent, are working hard to strengthen family ties and maintain family closeness. If you find yourself falling behind in some of these areas, it's never too late to make a fresh start with your adult children and your grandchildren.

Your best indication of the strength of your relationship with your grandchildren will come from them. Debbie Brown discovered how important she was to her twin grandsons during a recent visit. One of them told her, "Grandma, I wish you would move next door to us so that I could see you all the time." A little while later, the other twin said, "Grandma, I wish I could move into your house with you."

"I thought it was great that they both wanted more time with me, but they had entirely opposite solutions as to how that might be accomplished!" Debbie observed.

How Faith Can Help with Family Relationships

- Begin each day by thanking God for all the good things about your family.

- Give God all your fears and worries about family members.

- Be a forgiving person. Let go of anger and resentments that drag down you and your family members.

- Let go of unrealistic expectations. Accept family members for who they are.

- Remember that only God is perfect. Don't expect perfection from yourself or anyone else.

- Find ways to show family members and friends how much you appreciate them.

- Ask God to help you love each family member unconditionally.

- End each day by thanking God for all the good things in your life.

> We must be grateful that most people do value family relationships that are permanent and marked by mutual respect. They appreciate the Church's efforts to offer guidance and counseling in areas related to growth in love, overcoming conflict, and raising children.
>
> —Pope Francis, *Amoris Laetitia*, 38

Questions for Reflection

1. How would you describe what it means to be family?

2. In what ways do you work hard at maintaining close relationships with your grandchildren?

3. How does your Catholic faith support you in strengthening family ties?

Grandparent Prayer

Gracious and loving God, thank you for the members of my family. Give me everything I need to be a good grandparent. Give me patience and understanding when difficulties arise. Give me faith when I struggle with doubts. Give me hope when I am faced with disappointments. But most of all, Lord, give me love so that I can be present to each person in the family without holding anything back. Amen.

Chapter 11

Praying for Grandchildren

A priest suggested to Colette Byrne that, instead of worrying about her grandchildren, she pray to Jesus under his title as the Infant of Prague, a powerful Catholic devotion that has resulted in many graces and answered prayers for hundreds of years. Colette found a statue of the Infant and an information booklet that included a novena. She began praying an ongoing daily novena to the Infant for her grandchildren.

Several months later, Colette received a frantic telephone call, saying her nine-month-old grandson had been rushed to the hospital after being found floating in a swimming pool. Colette began praying with even greater intensity to the Infant of Prague. Her prayers were answered. "God is so good!" she recalls. "My grandson has no permanent damage, and today he is thriving."

In addition to praying a daily novena, Colette keeps a picture of her seven grandchildren on the windowsill above her kitchen sink. "I make the Sign of the Cross on their pictures and ask God to bless them as I do dishes or prepare meals," she says. "Pictures are a good reminder to pray."

The Power of Prayer

Prayer is one of the best things you can do for your grandchildren. Sometimes prayer is the only thing you can do. Prayer calms our fears, displaces worry, and relieves stress. Prayer changes our outlook on whatever problems or challenges our grandchildren might be facing.

Kim Doyle started a grandparent group in her parish that includes prayer. "We always end our meeting by praying for our grandchildren," she explains. "When you have others praying with you for your intentions, it is so powerful. Then we come back and share the changes for the positive that have happened as results of our prayers."

Offering It Up

Prayer also gives us the opportunity to unite whatever pain we may experience with the suffering of Jesus and offer it up for our grandchildren.

Joni Seith suffers from Ehlers-Danlos, a genetic connective tissue disease that can be quite painful. "When I have a bad episode, I offer it up for my son and my grandbaby, who both have the same disease," she explains. "I don't let any of my suffering go to waste. Knowing that it is going to them is where I find my joy."

Turning to Our Lady

When Sadie Fletcher's grandchildren were born, she gave each one of them to Our Lady. "I asked her to take care of them," she recalls. "They are her children. She is in charge. There might be something they are doing that I am worried about, but I know Our Lady will take care of it. There's nothing I can do, but there isn't anything that she can't do."

Many grandparents pray the Rosary for their grandchildren. Amanda Lauer remembers praying the Rosary in church for her daughter and daughter-in-law who were expecting babies two weeks apart. She had concerns because of some previous pregnancy issues. Amanda was looking directly at the statue of Our Lady as she prayed.

"When we got to the part in the prayer 'Blessed is the fruit of thy womb, Jesus,' I thought of my daughter and daughter-in-law," Amanda explains. "At that very moment, Mary looked right at me, and she said, 'Everything will turn out fine.' I was stunned. I looked at the other ladies to see what their reaction was, but none of the other women seemed to have heard it. After the Rosary, I lit a candle and asked Mary for her intercession on our behalf. I took one last look at her as I left church that day and thanked her for praying for us."

Amanda's grandson and granddaughter were both born healthy. "Ever since that time, when concerns come up in my life and our family's life, I repeat the words the Blessed Mother said to me in church that day, 'Everything will turn out fine.' Having that constant reminder and reassurance has been such a calming factor in my life."

When Prayer Seems Impossible

There are times in our lives when prayer is difficult. We may feel distracted or disconnected. One of the best techniques when prayer seems impossible is to turn your breathing into a prayer. You imagine that you are breathing in God's love as you inhale, then breathing out any worry or fear that you might feel. You can breathe in God's love and breathe out anger or frustration. You can breathe in God's love and imagine that love flowing through you. The more you practice this simple prayer, the easier it is to invite God's calming presence into your life.

A few minutes can be found each day to come together before the living God, to tell him our worries, to ask for the needs of our family, to pray for someone experiencing difficulty, to ask for help in showing love, to give thanks for life and for its blessings, and to ask Our Lady to protect us beneath her maternal mantle. With a few simple words, this moment of prayer can do immense good for our families.

—Pope Francis, *Amoris Laetitia*, 318

Questions for Reflection

1. In what ways do you pray for your grandchildren?

2. How has God answered your prayers?

3. How do your grandchildren respond when you explain that you are praying for them?

Grandparent Prayer

Kind and loving Lord, I humbly implore you to guide and protect my grandchildren. Shower them with your love. Keep them safe from all harm. Help them to grow in faith and in holiness. Amen.

—Chapter 12—

Sharing Faith

Fred and Fran Gilhoran love to share their Catholic faith with their eleven grandchildren. They are always on the lookout for teachable moments throughout the year.

"We light the Advent wreath," they explain. "We have our grandchildren put secret notes in their parents' shoes on the feast of St. Nicholas. We talk about Lent, the meaning of the word, the Lenten readings, and what we did as kids during Lent."

Sometimes Fred and Fran ask their grandchildren what they call "quiz questions" about the liturgical seasons or the Gospel reading for that Sunday. They take them to movies with moral value and discuss the movies afterward. They have also taken them to live performances of religious-themed musicals such as *Joseph and the Amazing Technicolor Dreamcoat*.

Fred and Fran like to talk about God. Whenever possible, they try to point out the beauty of God's creation. They also ask their grandchildren's opinions about what is happening in the news, so that they can reinforce Catholic values.

The Gilhorans are making a difference in their grandchildren's lives. But not all grandparents feel quite as comfortable—or are quite as effective—in sharing their faith.

Identifying the Difficulty

Many Catholic grandparents struggle with their ability to talk about faith with anyone—including grandchildren. Some grandparents say they don't know enough about their faith. They feel unsure of what to say or do because sharing faith was never part of their religious upbringing. They were taught that religion is personal and private.

A recent report from the Pew Research Center reveals that almost four out of every ten adults in the United States say they seldom (26 percent) or never (13 percent) discuss religion with anyone—not even members of their own families.[7]

On the other hand, there are Catholic grandparents who are so overzealous in sharing their faith that they push their children and grandchildren in the opposite direction. They talk too much about religion in ways that seem self-righteous and judgmental. They bombard family members on social media with religious images and messages. But the reality is that authentic faith sharing is not about pressuring anyone or trying to make family members feel guilty.

A Different Approach

Several years ago, a priest urged Deacon Gary Aitchison and his wife, Kay, to find some way for Catholic grandparents to develop a better connection with their grandchildren. Throughout their married lives, the Aitchisons were deeply involved in ministry to married couples as part of the Christian Family Movement (CFM).

"Most grandparents want to play a significant role in the lives of their grandchildren and are searching for the best ways to do it," Gary Aitchison explains. "We knew from personal experience how small-group sharing can transform people's lives."

So the Aitchisons combined their own experiences with the experiences of other grandparents and developed a six-session small-group discussion program entitled *The Grand Adventure: A New Call to Grandparenting*. Each session includes an opening prayer and Scripture reflection, a topic for discussion, and action ideas. *The Grand Adventure* also offers grandparents the opportunity for friendship and support.

"A lot of people tell us how important it was for them to go through this and how helpful it was," Kay Aitchison says.

An Awesome Experience

Kim Doyle used *The Grand Adventure* when she formed a grandparents group in her parish in Rosemount, Minnesota. "It was awesome," she recalled. "Each week *The Grand Adventure* gave us ideas on things we can do to form relationships with our grandchildren."

Kim explains that *The Grand Adventure* does not expect grandparents to teach their grandchildren the catechism or expound on the elements of the Catholic faith. Instead, *The Grand Adventure* shows grandparents how to strengthen their relationships with their grandchildren, and sharing faith takes place naturally through the way grandparents live their lives.

"The children are watching you, and your example is what they see," Kim explains. "If they see you praying the Rosary and they ask what it is, you can explain it to them. It's an introduction. It is slow and real. It isn't planned. The Holy Spirit opens the doors and gives us the opportunity to do his work. We just have to look at it from a different perspective."

Becoming a Role Model

The Aitchisons explain that the best way grandparents can witness to their faith is through their prayer life, their attendance at Mass, their friends, the types of entertainment they choose, their concern for the sufferings of others, their financial support

Sharing Faith

for good works, the religious items in their homes, the faith stories that they share, and the love that they show to everyone.

Fr. James Mallon, the host of the EWTN *Grandparents* video series, agrees. "Don't start the conversation with external faith practices like going to church," he advises. "That may have worked forty years ago. But people don't feel guilty about not going to church anymore. The idea that we should be shaped by duty or obligation is not even on their radar. Instead, speak to your grandchildren about your relationship with Jesus, your experience of prayer, and faith as something deep. Bring Jesus alive in how you live your faith. Often young people will come into the church through RCIA, and even though they weren't raised in the Church, the memory of their grandparents taking them to Mass or teaching them the Rosary or talking about prayer and the importance of faith in their lives is what inspired them."[8]

Other Ideas

Some grandparents pass on their Catholic faith in the gifts they give to their grandchildren. "When my granddaughter was making her First Communion," one woman told me, "I went to a Catholic store, and they told me I should buy a prayer book and a rosary separately. They decided not to sell First Communion sets anymore because kids won't wear a scapular. I thought about that, and it might be true, but I still wanted my granddaughter to know what a scapular is. So I went online and found a First Communion set with a scapular in it. When my granddaughter opened the set, she immediately asked what the scapular was, and I was able to explain it to her."

Increasingly, grandparents are asking the parents' permission to bring grandchildren to Mass. "In one family, the grandparents took the children to church, and the kids got involved in the parish," Gary Aitchison said. "After a few years, the parents started to go. The father wasn't a Catholic, and he joined the Church. Not every parent is going to allow their children to go to church with Grandma and Grandpa. But the invitation can always be there in a gentle way."

It is also becoming increasingly common for grandparents to bring their grandchildren to religious education classes, to sacramental formation, and to youth ministry programs in their parish. "It was a big sacrifice taking those kids to religious education, but it was worth it because both kids are rooted in their faith," one grandmother said.

Some grandparents pay tuition for Catholic schools. One grandmother volunteers as a school nurse in exchange for free tuition for her granddaughter. Another grandmother volunteers as a teacher's aide.

Transforming Ordinary Events

Joni Seith seizes the opportunity to turn ordinary events into chances to share faith. "If my grandchildren are disrespecting their mom, I jump on that and say, 'That's your mommy or daddy. You need to listen to them.' Respecting your parents is how you learn to respect God. I tell them there is an order in life—first God and then your parents. That's an important lesson in passing on the faith."

Gary and Kay Aitchison agree that grandparents need to be aware of the importance of sharing faith. "Sometimes we assume that kids know things, and they don't, so we have to share it with them," Kay explains. "I try to look for opportune times. You can't be overbearing, but I think you do the best you can, and you pray a lot!"

Some Ways to Share Your Faith

- Try to be present for sacramental milestones.

- Share memories—and photos—of the sacramental milestones in your life.

- Give your grandchildren religious gifts such as rosaries, Bibles, prayer books, prayer cards, statues, medals, crucifixes, and religious pictures.

- Tell stories about growing up Catholic.

- Take grandchildren to visit the parish you belonged to as a child.

- Tell your grandchildren about the little "miracles" that you have experienced.

- Read stories of the saints to your grandchildren.

- Plan a trip to a nearby shrine or monastery.

- Arrange to take your grandchildren for a tour of your local cathedral.

- Invite your grandchildren to special events in your parish, such as a May crowning, Christmas caroling, spaghetti dinners, and youth activities.

- Offer to babysit young grandchildren so that the parents can go to Mass together without distractions.

You are an important presence, because your experience is a precious treasure, which is essential if we would look to the future with hope and responsibility. Your maturity and wisdom, accumulated over the years, can help younger people in search of their own way, supporting them on the path of growth and openness to the future. The elderly, in fact, show that, even in the most difficult trials, one must never lose confidence in God and in a better future. They are like trees that continue to bear fruit: even under the weight of years, they can give their original contribution for a society rich in values and for the affirmation of the culture of life.

—Pope Francis, Speech to a Gathering of
Senior Citizens, October 15, 2016

Questions for Reflection

1. In what ways do you share your Catholic faith with your grandchildren?

2. How do you see yourself as a role model?

3. In what ways do you see your grandchildren growing in their faith?

Grandparent Prayer

Lord Jesus, send your Holy Spirit to show me the best ways to share my faith with my grandchildren. Allow them to see how much I treasure my relationship with you, Lord, and my connection to the Catholic Church. Make me an authentic witness to my faith. Amen.

Chapter 13

Praying with Grandchildren

Prayer is always woven into the time Chris and Bob Gill spend with their grandchildren. "We play Catholic school with the little ones," Chris explains. "We line up the stools in the kitchen and pretend we are on the bus going to school. Then we get off, hold hands, and say prayers—the Sign of the Cross, a Hail Mary, and a Glory Be. After that we go to the table, and school begins."

They pray again before meals. "We always say, 'Who should we pray for?' We give everybody a turn to mention someone. You'd be surprised how much a two-year-old loves to do that."

The Gills have a picture of the Blessed Mother hanging over their sofa. Chris encourages her grandchildren to stand on the couch and talk to Mary when they have a problem. "I swear, Mary's eyes look at those kids," Chris says. "Mary loves children, and the children learn the importance of praying."

During Lent, Bob and Chris take their grandchildren to church to pray the Stations of the Cross. "I go to each station," Chris says, "and I say, 'See, this is when Jesus falls. We feel bad when Jesus falls, just like when you get a boo-boo.' Or 'This is where Jesus meets his mommy. She is sad, and she is crying because Jesus is hurt.' Or 'This man's name is Simon, and he is helping Jesus, so we need to help people too.' We do the whole thing quickly, and the kids really love it because I try to relate it to their experiences."

In the evening, when Bob and Chris pray the Rosary, everyone in the family is invited to come over to their house to pray.

"The little ones can only handle about one mystery," Chris says. "I have toys on the table that they can play with. Then they pray the last mystery with us."

When someone is sick, the Gill family lays hands on them and prays for healing. "We have had tons of healings in our family," Chris says. "So the kids know the importance of being prayed over."

Teaching Grandchildren to Pray

There are no rules for teaching grandchildren how to pray. Each grandparent will have his or her own preferred style of prayer. Whatever style is most comfortable for you is the best style to share with your grandchildren.

"My first granddaughter was not being raised in any faith," one grandmother recalls. "Her other grandma used to teach her nursery songs. I started thinking, *If she can learn all these nursery songs, I can surely teach her prayers.* So I asked my son if it was okay, and he said yes. I started showing her how to make the Sign of the Cross, and I taught her basic prayers—the Our Father and the Hail Mary. Sure enough, she learned them."

Many grandparents teach their grandchildren the Guardian Angel Prayer: *Angel of God, my guardian dear, to whom God's love commits me here, ever this day be at my side, to light and guard, to rule and guide.*

"My granddaughter prays by just talking with God," one grandmother says. Other grandparents teach their grandchildren to sing songs to God. "My grandson loves to dance when we sing children's prayer songs," one grandmother says. "He also loves to do the hand gestures to songs like 'This Little Light of Mine.'"

Pope Francis used the Five-Finger Prayer with children when he was the archbishop of Buenos Aires.

- Start with the thumb, which is the closest finger to you, and pray for people you love.
- The pointer finger reminds you to pray for people who teach you and heal you.
- The middle finger is tallest and reminds us to pray for the leaders in our community and our country.
- The ring finger is the weakest and reminds us to pray for people in need.
- The pinkie finger is the smallest and reminds us to pray for ourselves.

Praying with the Saints

Veronica Cavan remembers the day she told her five-year-old grandson that whenever she loses something, she prays, "Help, St. Anthony! Please come around. Something is lost and can't be found." Her grandson looked baffled, so she went on to explain that when you ask a saint for something, the saint goes and asks God for you. "I could see the little wheels going in his head with the idea of intercession. But he got it. Now he knows a saint is very special to God, so he can ask a saint to pray for him."

Donna Kaiser and her grandchildren ask St. Francis of Assisi to take care of their pets. Donna also told her grandchildren that she prays to St. Monica for certain family members. "I encourage them to pray for them too," she explains. "One time we were passing the candles in church, and my youngest grandson asked to light a candle for those family members. My heart was melting!"

Other grandparents use books about saints, statues, holy cards, and medals to teach their grandchildren about praying with saints.

Laying a Foundation

No matter what kinds of prayers you teach your grandchildren, you are laying a foundation for their relationship with God. "It is important for the kids to know that God is number one in our lives and that everything revolves around him," says Joni Seith. "We built a little chapel in our house. The kids love being in there. They know it is a special place and that God is there in a special way."

Other grandparents set up prayer tables, with a crucifix, a Bible, and a candle. Reading Bible stories is a wonderful way to teach grandchildren to pray with Scripture. Some grandparents take their grandchildren on prayer walks—praying for the people in houses they pass if they walk through a neighborhood or thanking God for the beauty of creation if they walk in a park or through the woods.

Going to Mass together as a family is special for many grandparents. Some families follow up with a special meal afterward. It offers the opportunity to ask older grandkids how God spoke to them in the readings, the homily, the music, or their Communion meditation.

"On vacation we go to Mass and discuss how the church we visited might be different from ours but also so much alike," says Donna Kaiser. "There was one Mass our grandkids will always remember. The priest had his golden retriever come up the aisle with him. The dog stayed near the altar during Mass. After Mass the dog went around the church, picked up the hymnals, and dropped them into a basket. Not sure my grandchildren got a whole lot out of Mass, but it was unique!"

The Sign of the Cross

Making the Sign of the Cross is a Christian practice that began in the second century. It affirms our belief in the redemptive power of the crucified Christ. It is also a powerful invocation of the Holy Trinity because we make the Sign of the Cross "in the name of the Father, and of the Son, and of the Holy Spirit."

Here are some ideas for helping your grandchildren incorporate the Sign of the Cross into their prayer experiences:

- Use holy water to bless your grandchildren, making the Sign of the Cross on their foreheads.

- Let your grandchildren bless you.

- Make the Sign of the Cross before and after you say grace at mealtime.

- Point out the different ways the cross appears in church and during Mass, such as the cross on the altar cloths, the Lectionary, and the priest's vestments; the processional cross; crosses in the stained glass windows; crosses in the Stations of the Cross on the walls; the Sign of the Cross we make with holy water; and the Sign of the Cross the priest makes at the beginning of Mass, before the consecration, and during the final blessing.

- Tell your grandchildren that they were all marked with the Sign of the Cross on their foreheads when they were baptized.

- Explain that on Ash Wednesday, we receive ashes on our foreheads in the Sign of the Cross.

- Give your grandchildren small crosses to carry in their pockets as a reminder to pray.

I would like to ask you, dear families: Do you pray together from time to time as a family? Some of you do, I know. But so many people say to me: But how can we? . . . But in the family how is this done? After all, prayer seems to be something personal, and besides there is never a good time, a moment of peace. . . . Yes, all that is true enough, but it is also a matter of humility, of realizing that we need God, . . . all of us! We need his help, his strength, his blessing, his mercy, his forgiveness. And we need simplicity to pray as a family: simplicity is necessary! Praying the Our Father together, around the table, is not something extraordinary: it's easy. And praying the Rosary together, as a family, is very beautiful and a source of great strength! And also praying for one another. . . . This is what it means to pray in the family, and it is what makes the family strong: prayer.

Pope Francis, Homily, October 27, 2013

Questions for Reflection

1. How do you pray with your grandchildren?

2. What questions do your grandchildren ask about God or about prayer?

3. How has prayer strengthened your relationship with your grandchildren?

Grandparent Prayer:

Lord Jesus, when the apostles asked if you would teach them to pray, you gave them the words of the Our Father. Today I ask you to please teach me the best way to pray with my grandchildren. Allow your Holy Spirit to work through me to touch their hearts, their minds, and their souls. Amen.

Chapter 14

Why Didn't God Answer My Prayers? (and Other Tough Questions Grandchildren Ask)

Even before his mother was pregnant, five-year-old Patrick Cavan, who already had a little brother, told everyone that next time he was going to get a sister. When the new baby was on the way and a sonogram showed that it was a boy, Patrick was confused.

"I don't understand," he told his grandmother. "I wanted a sister, and I prayed to God for a sister. The first time I wanted a sister, I got Gregory. This time I wanted a sister, and I am getting another brother."

"God doesn't make mistakes," Veronica Cavan told her grandson. "There must be some reason that God wants you to have another brother."

Patrick accepted her answer. "I couldn't think of anything else to say," Veronica admits.

After the new baby was born, Patrick forgot all about his disappointment. "Now he adores Nicholas," Veronica says. "Patrick loves babies."

Answering Tough Questions

Grandparents are often the ones children come to with questions when things in their lives don't make sense to them. How grandparents answer those questions can make a profound impact on their grandchildren.

Sometimes it's not entirely clear what a child wants to know. Young children are often inclined to ask a complex question when they are seeking a simple answer. One grandparent recalled the day her grandson asked, "What is a credit card?" She went into a long explanation about how you use credit cards when you don't have money, and then you pay the bill later.

"Oh," her grandson replied. "I thought a credit card was a rectangle."

Chagrined, the grandmother realized her grandson was asking about shapes—not finances!

It's not always easy to decipher a child's questions. It can help to probe a little before answering, saying something along the lines of "Tell me more about what you want to know." Or "Is there something specific about this that you want to know?"

Most of the time, you probably have to go with the flow and answer the best way you know how. Here are some of the toughest questions that grandparents might be asked:

- **Questions about Their Parents**

If there is a lot of stress in the family, young children might ask why Mommy or Daddy is mad all the time. Older children might ask if Mommy and Daddy are going to get a divorce. What they are seeking is not information as much as affirmation. Comfort them by saying that you love them and that their parents love them. Assure them that they have done nothing wrong. Suggest that you say a prayer together for their family.

- **Questions about You**

If there has been a recent death in the family, your grand-children might be afraid that you are also going to die. Explain that everybody has to die when they are finished with what-ever God wants them to do in this world. Assure them that you hope to be with them for a long time. Suggest that you say a prayer that everyone in the family stays healthy and holy.

- **Questions about Themselves**

Kids can be competitive, and they sometimes wonder if you like them better than your other grandchildren. Even if you do have a secret favorite, it is best to deflect this question by pointing out that each of your grandchildren is different and that you love all of them for the unique people that they are. Older grandchildren might ask more specific questions, such as whether you think she is smart or whether you think he is funny. Try to find out the reason for this question and whether some person or situation triggered it. You might find yourself in a deeper discussion about bullying or feelings of insecurity. Remind your grandchildren that they are all children of God. Pray together to reinforce in their minds the fact that God has unconditional love for them.

- **Questions about Why God Allows Bad Things to Happen**

Young children are probably focused on a specific situation when they ask a question like this, and you can probe a little to figure out exactly what they need to hear before you answer the question. With older kids, the question can be more complicated, and the answers are not always easy to understand or to accept. You can tell them that God has given us the gift of free will, and sometimes suffering is a consequence when people do bad things—purposely or accidentally.

Furthermore, you can tell them that God allowed people to kill Jesus, and then God made something better happen when he brought Jesus back to life on Easter Sunday. If God transformed the suffering of Jesus, God can also bring something good out of any suffering—even if the suffering is caused by a fluke of nature or a twist of fate. Ask your grandchildren to join you in praying that God will help them believe—even if bad things happen—that something good will come out of it.

Veronica Cavan advises grandparents to answer questions in ways grandchildren can understand. "They have to know that you are not afraid to share your thoughts—especially when they have questions," she says. "You can't force your beliefs on them, but that shouldn't stop you from sharing. Be who you are. You can't lie to them. You can't put them off. It's important to show that you believe God is in your daily life by saying things like 'I prayed to God about that' or 'You can ask St. Patrick to help you.' You can show them that your faith is not just something you do on Sunday, but it's part of your daily life."

Ground Rules for Answering Tough Questions

- Don't undermine the parents' authority.

- Always answer the question as simply as possible.

- Don't ever lie or try to twist the truth.

- Admit when you don't know the answer.

- Acknowledge your grandchild's feelings.

- Be prepared to answer the same question over and over.

- Try to offer reassurance in whatever you say.

A young person once asked me—you know how young people ask hard questions!—"Father, what did God do before he created the world?" Believe me, I had a hard time answering that one. I told him what I am going to tell you now. Before he created the world, God was in love, because God is love. The love he had within himself, the love between the Father and the Son, in the Holy Spirit, was so great, so overflowing—I'm not sure if this is theologically precise, but you will get what I am saying—that love was so great that God could not be selfish. He had to go out from himself, in order to have someone to love outside of himself. So God created the world.
—Pope Francis, Address, September 26, 2015

Questions for Reflection

1. What are some of the questions your grandchildren have asked?

2. How do you respond when you don't have an answer to your grandchild's question?

3. What was the most difficult question a grandchild ever asked you?

Grandparent Prayer

Lord, give me the wisdom, the knowledge, and the patience to answer my grandchildren's tough questions. Help me recognize when I have offered a good answer and when I may need outside assistance to help them. Make me always conscious of the complexities they face in their lives. Allow me to be someone in whom they can trust and confide. Amen.

Chapter 15

Avoiding Pitfalls

When Nancy Allaire Donohue answered the telephone, a young male voice said, "Grams?" At first Nancy was confused because her grandchildren call her "Nanna." But she had been thinking about her grandson that morning, and she blurted out, "Is this R. J.?"

"Yes," came the reply. "I have some bad news. I'm in Toronto, and I was in an automobile accident."

Panic-stricken, Nancy asked if he was all right. "I have a broken nose, and I need your help," he replied. "Could you send me $2,000?"

Nancy felt paralyzed. "My mind isn't thinking right," she told him. "I don't know how I can get the money to you."

When he suggested that she could give him her credit card number, Nancy immediately told him that he had to call his parents. "They can't help me," he replied, "and I can see now that you can't help me either, so I'm going to have to find someone else." Click. He hung up the phone.

Afterward, Nancy realized it had been a scam. "The good news is that I didn't give out my credit card number. The sad news is that people are doing these horrible things. If I had a heart condition, I could have had a heart attack during that call. How cruel that people do that!"

How Love Can Hurt

It is cruel for scam artists to prey on the emotions of grandparents. Initially, Nancy's deep love and concern for her grandson blinded her to what was happening. The only thing that inadvertently saved Nancy was the firm belief that the parents come first and should always be contacted in case of an emergency. "I love my grandson," Nancy explains, "but in my subconscious, I know my place."

It seems almost inconceivable that loving a grandchild could cause problems for them or for us. But unfortunately, it can and does happen. Sometimes we love our grandchildren so much, and we are so proud of them, that we inadvertently do things that we should not do.

Here are some of the most common pitfalls grandparents face out of a misguided sense of love for a grandchild:

- **Offering Treats**

We all want our grandchildren to be happy, but don't ever give them candy or toys or treats without their parents' permission. It's so easy to say to ourselves, "Another cookie won't hurt," but another cookie might hurt if it disturbs the child's ability to go down for a nap or to eat dinner. "I found out that even something as simple as allowing grandchildren to lick the beaters when I am making cookies could become an issue," one grandmother said. "I didn't realize that raw eggs in the batter can cause salmonella poisoning."

- **Showing Them Off**

We are all proud of our grandchildren, but don't show them off to your friends unless their parents approve of what you're doing. A grandmother was babysitting her four-year-old granddaughter one afternoon and took the little girl with her when she stopped in at a wake. The grandmother wanted to show off her granddaughter to all her friends. Later that evening, the child told her parents that she met all of Grandma's friends, and one of them was sleeping in a big box. The parents were furious.

- **Not Being Fair**

You may feel closer to one grandchild or to one set of grandchildren, but don't ever show your feelings in the things you say or do. "I had a friend who idolized a granddaughter who lived out of town," one grandmother recalls. "She had all kinds of photos of the little girl, and she talked incessantly about what this little girl was doing at home and in school. The other grandchildren hated her for it."

- **Giving Too Many Gifts**

We all love to give our grandchildren surprises, but don't go overboard with gift giving. Always ask the parents before you go on a shopping spree. If the parents ask you to cut back on the number of gifts or on how much the gifts cost, honor their wishes. One grandmother found a great compromise when her granddaughter wanted $200 sneakers for Christmas. "Okay," she said, "I talked to your parents, and they agreed that your aunts and I can pool our money and buy the sneakers, but this will be the only gift that you will get from us this Christmas."

- **Undermining the Parents' Discipline**

You might think the parents are being too hard on your grandchild, but it is not your place to undermine the restrictions they place on the child for bad behavior. One grandfather got into trouble with his son whenever his grandchild was put into time out. "He didn't mean to do it," the grandfather would say. His grandson got the message that he could do anything he wanted when Grandpa was around.

- **Disrespecting the Parents' Wishes**

You may not agree with the way the children are being raised, and you can make your opinion known to the parents privately, but you have no right to disregard their wishes. It may be something as monumental as what religion your grandchildren will be raised in, or it may be as insignificant as whether they will believe in the tooth fairy. "My grandchildren are being raised as vegetarians," one grandparent said. "As much as I would love to take them out for a hot dog, I wouldn't dare."

John Mitchell, grandfather of eight, offers the following advice for avoiding pitfalls. "Always defer to the parents, even when you know that you have a better way!" he says. "And pray for these—and all—situations, because God will show you how to proceed."

Letting Go

Many of us operate under the illusion that we are in control. Becoming a good grandparent shatters that illusion and forces us to accept the fact that we are not in control of our children or our grandchildren. We are called to let go.

Letting go does not mean that we stop loving our children or our grandchildren. It doesn't mean that we stop caring. It means that, even when our ways of doing things might be better, we respect the rights of the parents to make decisions for their children. Refusing to let go almost always leads to hurt feelings, anger, and resentments.

The process of letting go is at the core of authentic spirituality. We let go when we trust that God is watching over our family and that everything will work out for the best. The question we have to ask ourselves is whether our faith in God is strong enough to overcome whatever desire we have to be in control.

> I thank God that many families, which are far from considering themselves perfect, live in love, fulfill their calling and keep moving forward, even if they fall many times along the way.
>
> —Pope Francis, *Amoris Laetitia*, 57

Questions for Reflection

1. In what ways can love for a grandchild become an excuse for our own selfish desires?

2. What are some of the pitfalls you try to avoid as a grandparent?

3. How difficult is it for you to let go of your desire to be in control?

Grandparent Prayer

Good and gracious God, give me the courage to let go of the desire to do things my way. Help me understand that in letting go, I place my grandchildren in your loving care. I trust that you will guide and protect them. Amen.

Chapter 16

What Makes Your Grandchild Special?

We all think of our grandchildren as special. They all have gifts and talents that make them unique. But grandparents would be well advised to watch the words they use when telling grandchildren how special they are!

The problem is that telling grandchildren that they are "special" is a half-truth. The real reason we are special is because God gives each of us special gifts and talents. It's not about us; it's about what God has given to us!

For example, you can explain to young grandchildren that God has given us

- eyes so we can see;
- ears so we can hear;
- a mouth so we can speak;
- hands so we can do things;
- feet so we can go places;
- a mind so we can think;
- a heart so we can love.

But emphasize to your grandchildren that these physical gifts are not given for our own glory. God wants us to use our gifts to help each other and to make the world a better place.

Unique Gifts and Talents

God also gives unique gifts and talents to individuals. Maybe your grandchild is smart or athletic or has a talent for music, art, or writing. Some children are natural leaders. Some children deeply care about other people. Some have a gift for nurturing plants or animals. "I was at a Catholic workshop one time, and the speaker told us never to ask a grandchild what they want to do when they grow up," one grandmother said. "Instead, he told us to ask our grandchildren how they will use the gifts God has given them when they grow up."

You can help your grandchildren understand that a gift can also be a weakness. For example, a grandchild who has a gift of physical strength should never use it to bully someone. A grandchild who can make people laugh should never use humor to belittle someone.

Nor should we ever be jealous of someone else's gift. Encourage your grandchildren to celebrate everyone's gifts, because gifts are like pieces of a puzzle. We can't see the picture unless all the pieces fit together.

The Spiritual Gifts

With older grandchildren, you can explore the spiritual gifts that each person receives at Baptism and that are strengthened through the Sacrament of Confirmation.

- Wisdom allows them to see the world as God sees it.
- Understanding helps them to realize that sometimes truth lies beneath the surface.
- Judgment allows them to know the difference between what is right and what is wrong.

- Knowledge gives them the desire to learn.
- Reverence helps them appreciate what is holy.
- Wonder and awe give them a deeper appreciation of the mysteries in life.

Talking with grandchildren about their gifts is one of the easiest ways to share your Catholic faith. Children are almost always excited to learn more about themselves. With older grandkids, you can even do a little Internet research on spiritual gifts and talents.

Sharing Your Gifts

Look for opportunities to share your own special gifts and talents with your grandchildren.

"I was a pastry chef," Peter Konieczny says. "I bake all kinds of cakes for family baptisms, First Communions, confirmations, and birthdays. My grandchildren would watch me when they were little, and they helped me as they got older."

"I do a lot of crocheting and quilting," says Yolanda Sosa. "I made quilts for each one of my grandchildren."

Your conversations with your grandchildren about God-given gifts and talents may be one of the best gifts you ever give to them or to yourself.

Talking about God-Given Gifts

- Have your grandchildren join you in asking the Holy Spirit to help you identify the gifts given to each child in your family.

- Read stories about the saints, and look for ways they used their gifts.

- Explore ways your grandchildren can use their gifts at home or at school.

- Remind your grandchildren that God expects them to use their gifts for good.

- Encourage your grandchildren to thank God every day for the gifts he has given to them.

> The Lord does not give the same things to everyone in the same way: He knows us personally and entrusts us with what is right for us; but in everyone, in all, there is something equal: the same, immense trust. God trusts us, God has hope in us!
> —Pope Francis, Angelus, November 16, 2014

Questions for Reflection

1. Think about your grandchildren's God-given gifts and talents. In what ways are they different from your gifts and talents? In what ways are they the same?

2. How are you using your God-given gifts and talents as a grandparent?

3. Reflect on how your grandchildren's God-given gifts could someday be used to help build up the body of Christ.

Grandparent Prayer

Lord Jesus, send down your Holy Spirit to inspire me as I help my grandchildren discover their gifts and talents. Show them how they can use their gifts in ways that are pleasing to you. Keep my grandchildren humble. Give them the strength and the courage they need to always use their gifts for good. Amen.

Chapter 17

Grandparents of Tweens and Teens

Rose Mary Buscaglia has ten grandchildren, and she understands firsthand the challenges of being a Catholic grandparent as grandchildren become adolescents and young adults.

"When they are little, you can teach them things like the Rosary, and to say their prayers, and to bless everybody at night, and to say grace before meals," she says. "But when they come into those teenage years, it's a very fine line as to whether teenagers will listen to you. You can still talk to them about faith, but you have to continually stay tuned to their lives and be able to recognize the moments when you can discuss faith."

Rose Mary recalls one conversation with her oldest grandson who had just recovered from a serious illness. When her grandson asked why she thought he had survived without any residual effects, Rose Mary replied, "I like to think it was because of our prayers and our faith. I did a lot of praying for you, and that's what faith is."

Her statement led to a deeper conversation about how faith is not always easy. Her grandson said that the topic of Nazi Germany came up in school because a ninety-year-old former Nazi was being tried for his actions in a concentration camp. Her grandson wondered if maybe this man was forced to do those horrible things to protect his family. "That's a possibility," Rose Mary acknowledged, "but this is when our faith helps us through tough decisions about what is right and what is wrong."

The following year, when Rose Mary asked her grandson if there was anything specific that she had done to help him with his faith, he said, "Yes. You are open, honest, and knowledgeable. I can always ask you questions."

An Evolving Relationship

A recent study of grandparents and teenage grandchildren, funded by the Centre of Research on Families and Relationships and the Economic and Social Research Council in Scotland, showed that Rose Mary's experiences with her grandson are typical. When grandchildren are younger, grandparents spend more time on simple activities. As grandchildren move closer to their teen years, their relationship with their grandparents focuses more on talking, asking questions, and seeking support. In this study, both grandparents and teenage grandchildren agreed that listening was important. The teens admitted that they could share concerns with grandparents that they might not discuss with their parents.[9]

Rose Mary acknowledges how difficult life can be for teens in today's society because of all the mixed messages they receive. "Prestige, success, and money have replaced what is really important—family values and caring about other people," she says.

She tells her tween and teen grandchildren that faith is very personal. "Faith is your relationship with God. I tell them that sometimes your relationship with God is open, and sometimes it is private, but that's okay. There are going to be times in your life when things might get rough, but you can still have that connection with God. You can still have prayer in your life."

A Developing Faith

Rose Mary understands that it is normal for adolescents to wrestle with what they believe. This time of their lives is a very important stage in their faith journey, carrying them from childhood faith, which is essentially the unquestioning acceptance of their family's faith, to adult faith, in which they make a mature, personal commitment to Jesus Christ and the Catholic Church. This transition period can be very unsettling for tweens and teens. They essentially ask themselves, "Am I Catholic because my family is Catholic, or is this something that I really believe?"

How Grandparents Can Help

Grandparents who want to help their tween and teen grandchildren through this faith transition need to be prepared for tough questions. It may sound at times as if your grandchildren are questioning God or the Church or your family values. You don't have to be defensive. You don't have to supply all the answers to their questions. Most of the time, you just need to listen. But there are also times when it is important for you to share your opinions and your experiences.

Sometimes the best thing grandparents can do is to live their faith in such a way that their grandchildren see that faith gives meaning to life. "My grandchildren see us going to Mass and serving as Eucharistic ministers," one grandfather says. "They see how we reach out when someone is in crisis. They see that because we have faith, we are happier and more peaceful than families of their friends who do not have faith."

Dr. Karl Pillemer, a research professor at Cornell University, says that "as many as nine out of ten adult grandchildren feel their grandparents influenced their values and behaviors.

Grandparents transmit to their grandchildren the values and norms of social order."[10]

Keeping in Touch

Marilyn Henry advises grandparents of tweens and teens, "Meet them where they are. That means you might have to text them. I text a lot. When my granddaughter was moving into a college dorm, I texted, 'I'm praying for you!'"

Last Valentine's Day, Marilyn sent a group text to her grandchildren, saying, "Whoever sends me back a text about St. Valentine—and it can't be the same facts that your cousin just sent—I will send you something in the mail." They all looked up St. Valentine, and Marilyn sent them gift cards. "It was wonderful for me because I learned some things too. Don't miss those opportunities."

Pope Francis acknowledges that e-mails, text messages, and social networks can be valuable forms of communication. "It is not technology which determines whether or not communication is authentic, but rather the human heart and our capacity to use wisely the means at our disposal" (Message, World Communications Day, January 24, 2016).

What Kind of Example Do You Set for Your Grandchildren?

It doesn't take long for tween and teen grandchildren to notice discrepancies between what you say and what you do. Here are some questions to ponder:

- Do you expect your grandchildren to control their tempers but lose your temper when something goes wrong?

- Do you expect your grandchildren to follow the rules but make excuses for times when you break a rule?

- Do you teach your grandchildren to tell the truth but exaggerate to make a story more dramatic?

- Do you tell little white lies to avoid doing something that you don't want to do?

- Do you tell your grandchildren how important it is to pray but never let them see you pray?

- Do you tell your grandchildren that it is important to go to Mass and then complain about the priest, the length of the homily, or the people in your parish?

- Do you tell your grandchildren not to use profanity but take the Lord's name in vain when you're upset or angry?

- Do you teach your grandchildren to be nice to everyone and then hold grudges against other people?

- Do you teach your grandchildren the importance of following through on what they say they're going to do and then fail to keep your promises?

Chances are you've recognized yourself in one or more of these questions. Don't despair! No one is perfect. But it's important to recognize that you can be better. Ask God to help, "for God is at work in you, both to will and to work for his good pleasure" (Philippians 2:13).

There is no lack of young people who are very generous, supportive, and committed at the religious and social level; young people who seek a true spiritual life; young people who hunger for something different from what the world has to offer. There are wonderful young people, and not just a few. But among young people there are also victims of the logic of *worldliness*, which can be summarized as follows: the search for success at any price, for easy money and easy pleasure. This logic also seduces many young people. Our task can be none other than that of standing beside them to infect them with the joy of the Gospel and of belonging to Christ.
—Pope Francis, Address, January 28, 2017

Questions for Reflection

1. In what ways do your tween and teen grandchildren struggle with their faith?

2. What kinds of questions about faith or life have they asked you?

3. How do you share your Catholic faith with your tween and teen grandchildren?

Grandparent Prayer

Lord God, help me to remember my own tween and teen struggles so that I can support my grandchildren during this important time in their lives. Give me the insight to know when to speak and when to listen. Allow me to be an instrument of your love and compassion. Amen.

—*Chapter 18*—

Listening with Your Heart

Marianna Konieczny recalls the day she was in the garden with her grandchildren and one of them said, "Remember the story you told us about hear and listen? You told us hearing is when you hear some bell ringing or some noise. But when you listen, you open your heart and look into the person's eyes. That's the difference."

Marianna was thrilled that her grandchildren had gotten the message. "Listening is really important because it makes them feel as if you really care about them," she says. "Listening is from the heart."

The Art of Listening

Grandparents can practice the art of listening from the time their grandbabies begin to babble. Looking into their eyes and commenting on the sounds they make helps infants develop language and communication skills. Even little babies can see from the expression on your face and the tone of your voice that you care about them.

"I remember that when my children were infants and just starting to smile and make noises, my mother would encourage them by saying things like 'Tell me more' or 'I love your stories,'" one grandmother says. "So I try to do that with my grandbabies."

As babies become toddlers, listening becomes even more important. Seventy-five percent of a child's brain development takes place during the first two years of life. Listening to a child who is beginning to form words and ideas encourages them to talk—especially if they exhibit some difficulty in expressing themselves. Affirm your grandchildren by repeating their words.

"My grandson is just learning to talk, and I have a very difficult time understanding what he says sometimes," one grandfather admits. "So I say things to him like 'Oh, really! Tell me more about that!'"

Once they enter preschool, most grandchildren have plenty to say. "I ask about their school, their teachers, the rules, their friends, the new things they are learning, and the fun things they are doing," a grandmother says.

Listening as preschool children sing their songs or recite their poems is another way to affirm the importance of what they are learning. It's a good idea to encourage children to share the richness of their imaginations. Invite them to tell you about their hopes and their dreams.

As children enter grade school, let them know that you are a "safe" person and that you can be trusted to keep a confidence if they need to talk. Be especially alert to any concerns or fears they might express. Whether they are complaining about something trivial or wrestling with a major problem, it is important for children to understand that talking about something that is troubling them is a good way to find a solution to a problem.

Don't share what they tell you with their parents, unless you have their permission to do so. In situations in which you are concerned about a grandchild's health or safety, you should express your concern to the child, tell them it's time to involve a parent, and assure them that you can be present when they talk with their parents.

As children approach their teenage years, ask their opinions about things that are happening in your family, your community, your parish, and the world. Let them know that you value their thoughts and insights.

The Joy of Listening

One of the added benefits of listening to your grandchildren is discovering a whole new world of information and ideas. "My grandchildren are always opening my eyes to something," one grandfather says. "I sometimes get stuck in my senior citizen way of thinking, but they break through that with something brand new. It keeps me fresh. They always amaze me!"

Becoming a Better Listener

Here are a few helpful hints on honing your listening skills:

- **Pay attention to what your grandchild is saying.**

This is not as simple as it sounds. The average person speaks at a rate of one hundred to two hundred words per minute, but rates can reach five hundred words per minute. You might have to really concentrate if you want to keep up with a fast-talking grandchild!

- **Don't interrupt.**

Let your grandchild tell the story without breaking their train of thought. Don't feel the need to talk if your grandchild pauses. A moment of silence sometimes gives both of you a chance to collect your thoughts.

- **Be aware of your body language.**

Make eye contact. Don't give the impression that you are bored. Don't ever try to do something else while you're supposed to be listening.

- **Respond.**

Use statements that reinforce the child, such as "What I hear you saying is . . . " or "It sounds like you are . . . " Keep in mind that you don't always need words to show your grandchild that you are listening. Tears, laughter, sighs, a nod of your head, or a hug also shows that you care and are paying attention.

> We can be fully present to others only by giving fully of ourselves and forgetting all else. Our loved ones merit our complete attention. Jesus is our model in this, for whenever people approached to speak with him, he would meet their gaze, directly and lovingly (cf. Mark 10:21).
> —Pope Francis, *Amoris Laetitia*, 323

Questions for Reflection

1. What are some of your experiences of listening to your grandchildren?

2. What have you learned by listening?

3. In what ways could you strengthen your listening skills?

Grandparent Prayer

Open my ears, Lord, and allow me to listen to my grandchildren with my heart. Help them to realize that listening is a manifestation of my love and respect for them. When the need for me to talk arises, send forth your Holy Spirit to inspire my words in ways that will touch their minds and their hearts. Amen.

Chapter 19

Forgiveness

When Joni Seith's daughter came to pick up her son, she asked, "How was he? Was he good?" Joni replied, "He was perfect."

But Joni admits there are times when her grandson is not perfect—like the times he is not nice to his little sister. When that happens, Joni deals with it. "I'll say, 'What's the problem? Why are you picking on your sister?' Then we talk about it."

As much as we want to believe that our grandchildren are perfect, we know that they are going to make mistakes. They are going to say and do things that hurt other people. They are going to have to learn how to ask for forgiveness. And they are going to have to learn how to forgive.

Throughout the Gospels, Jesus emphasizes the importance of forgiveness. When Peter asked if it is enough to forgive seven times, Jesus told him to forgive seventy times seven times (Matthew 18:22). Jesus assured us that if we forgive, we will be forgiven our own failings (6:14). On the cross, Jesus gave us an example of forgiveness when he prayed, "Father, forgive them; for they know not what they do" (Luke 23:34).

Forgiveness Is Good for Us

When we seek forgiveness, we admit that we were wrong, we accept responsibility for what we have done, and we learn from the experience so that we don't make the same mistake again. When we forgive, we acknowledge that we have been hurt, but we choose to let go of anger, resentment, and negative thoughts that can harden our hearts and make us bitter.

Chances are your grandchildren are already learning powerful lessons about forgiveness—not by anything you've said, but by how you've dealt with difficult situations in your own life. Sometimes, however, we inadvertently pass on attitudes and behaviors that are not very good models of forgiveness. For example:

- We hold grudges.
- We use the silent treatment instead of talking things over.
- We avoid the person who hurt us instead of dealing with the problem.
- We give excuses for our actions instead of apologizing.
- We blame others for something we did wrong.
- We bring up the past offenses of others.
- We refuse to forgive ourselves for our own past mistakes.

If any of this sounds familiar, decide now to change these attitudes and behaviors before you pass them on to your grandchildren. Look for little things that happen in everyday life, and use those incidents to give your grandchildren a positive understanding of forgiveness.

The Right Way to Apologize

"My grandson is always saying he's sorry when he does something wrong," one grandmother said. "But I don't think he really understands why he is saying he is sorry. I think he says it so that he can be released from time-out."

A lot of people struggle with making a sincere apology, so it is even more challenging when you try to teach a grandchild the importance of asking for forgiveness. The first step is to make sure your grandchild understands that what they did is wrong. For example, you must identify the behavior: "*It is wrong to hit somebody.*" "*It is wrong to take another child's toy.*" "*It is wrong to call someone a name.*"

The next step is crucial: help your grandchild recognize how they would feel if that bad thing had been done to them. Don't pose this as a question. Instead, make a statement such as "*You would feel hurt or you would cry if someone did that to you.*"

Then you can help your grandchild learn to apologize sincerely. Something along the lines of "*I was wrong. I am sorry I did that to you. I won't do it again.*" You can reinforce the apology by suggesting that you and your grandchild pray for the person who was hurt.

Learning to ask for forgiveness is important. But there is another side to this coin. Our grandchildren are also going to be in situations where they are hurt by things that other people say and do. They are going to have to learn how to forgive.

Learning to Forgive

It is impossible for children to forgive while they are still hurt, angry, or crying. Give your grandchild a chance to calm down. Then ask what happened and how they feel about what happened.

If another child comes over to apologize, you can make sure that child understands that what they did was wrong. You can even allow your grandchild to express indignation: "*I don't like it when you do that to me!*"

Sometimes the problem can be solved with the righting of the wrong, such as the return of the toy that was taken. Then your grandchild can forgive the offender, and everyone goes back to playing nicely. But sometimes, especially when there was physical or emotional pain, forgiveness becomes more complex.

Children should never be abused by other children—no matter how young or old they are. Sometimes it's right to remove your grandchild from the situation. Sometimes it is a matter of talking with the parents of the other child. Sometimes talking directly to the offending child is appropriate.

"We were at the playground, and an older kid started kicking my five-year-old grandson," one grandmother recalled. "I put a stop to it immediately. I told the older child, 'Don't you ever kick my grandson or any other child at this playground again.' The older kid slinked away, and I suggested to my grandson that we forgive him by saying a prayer for him. My grandson was able to put the whole incident behind him."

Dealing with Bullies

It's a different story when a child is being constantly bullied. Sometimes children will tell a grandparent they are being bullied before saying anything to anyone else. Explain to your grandchild that bullying is a serious matter and that you need to talk about this with their parents. Most day cares, preschools, elementary schools, and high schools have procedures to follow in situations regarding bullies. Your grandchild may eventually reach a point where he or she can forgive a bully, but it won't happen until the bullying behavior stops.

The Beauty of Forgiveness

When we forgive—no matter what age we are—we make a conscious decision to let go of the hurt. We forgive because forgiveness frees us from anger, resentment, frustration, and thoughts of revenge. Forgiveness restores spiritual, mental, and emotional wholeness. Without forgiveness, bitterness takes control of our lives. It hardens our hearts. It affects our prayer life, our relationships, our thought processes, and our health.

"I asked my grandson to forgive me because I had to cancel a fishing date we had planned," one grandfather said. "He told me that I had hurt his heart. I explained to him why I couldn't go fishing. I told him I was also sad, and I was very sorry. He hugged me and said it was okay. We went fishing the following week."

Creating an Atmosphere of Forgiveness

Here are some suggestions on how you can help your grandchildren learn the importance of forgiveness:

- Assure your grandchildren that it's okay to tell you if something that you've said or done hurts their feelings.

- Apologize to your grandchildren when you do something that hurts them.

- Give your grandchildren the words to use when they need to apologize: *"I'm sorry I hurt you." "I shouldn't have done that." "Please forgive me."*

- Teach your grandchildren the importance of graciously accepting someone else's apology.

- Share with your grandchildren examples of times when you've forgiven someone who has hurt you.

- Share examples of times when you've had to ask for forgiveness.

- Teach your grandchildren to say an Our Father for the people who have hurt them.

- Talk to your children about how much better you feel after forgiving someone or after receiving forgiveness.

Forgiveness is not always easy. But it is always the right thing to do. It is one of the most important lessons your grandchildren will ever learn, because it is closely connected to the ability to love and be loved.

One cannot live without seeking forgiveness, or at least, one cannot live at peace, especially in the family. We wrong one another every day. We must take into account these mistakes, due to our frailty and our selfishness. However, what we are asked to do is to promptly heal the wounds that we cause, to immediately reweave the bonds that break within the family. If we wait too long, everything becomes more difficult.
—Pope Francis, Audience, November 4, 2015

Questions for Reflection

1. How have you had to help your grandchildren ask for forgiveness?

2. How have you had to help your grandchildren forgive?

3. In what ways do you show your grandchildren the importance of forgiveness?

Grandparent Prayer

Merciful and loving God, help my grandchildren to understand the need to forgive and to be forgiven. Give me the courage to embrace forgiveness in my own life so that I can be an authentic role model for them. Amen.

—*Chapter 20*—

Family Traditions

Maryann Szafran has always treasured her Polish family traditions. She remembers making pierogi with her mother and her grandmother. From the time her own granddaughters turned five, Maryann included them in the pierogi making. "Those were fun times, with lots of flour all over the floor and very misshaped pierogis," Maryann recalls. "To this day, we all work together making them, and on Christmas Eve, we are very proud of our efforts."

When Maryann was growing up, Christmas Eve was a day of abstinence for Catholics, which meant no meat. "So our menu always included fish and potato pancakes," she explains. "We still enjoy the same menu."

Maryann also loves the Christmas Eve tradition of sharing the *oplatek*—a thin wafer with a texture similar to the hosts used for Communion at Mass—with family members before dinner. "We are an emotional family, so there are always tears as we all share our good wishes and love as we break this wafer with each other," she explains. "My granddaughters are teenagers, and they still insist on these traditions."

Something Special

Christmas is a special time, associated with many traditions. Family members make favorite recipes that have been handed down from generation to generation. Some families eat tamales on Christmas Eve. Others enjoy the Sicilian seven-fish dinner. Maybe your family eats pickled herring or oyster stew. For some families, the dinner might not be as important as the sugar cookies cut into shapes and frosted.

"We always have red Jell-O with real whipped cream on Christmas Eve," one grandmother says. "It's not really that special to most people, but it was a tradition that my great-grandmother started, and it is special to us."

Actually, the type of food your family eats doesn't matter. In fact, a tradition doesn't have to have anything to do with food. It could be a custom or ritual that your family carries out year after year.

"Our family cuts down Christmas trees together every year," one grandfather related. "Then our grandkids come back to our house to help us decorate our tree."

"I take my grandchildren out every year to do their Christmas shopping," a grandmother says.

A Sense of Belonging

Traditions bind family members together and instill a sense of belonging. Children learn important lessons from family traditions—about personal values, social behaviors, and communication skills. Even when families disagree at family gatherings, children learn valuable lessons about respecting others and dealing with conflict.

"We have a big family," one grandfather acknowledges, "and there are always differences of opinion. Sometimes the discussions can get quite spirited. But in the end, we always agree that even if we don't see eye to eye, we are still a family, and we will always love each other."

Family traditions help your grandchildren feel safe and secure within the family structure. As they get older, your grandchildren are likely to remember your family traditions more than the gifts you gave them.

"I asked my granddaughter who gave her a particular gift for her birthday, and she couldn't remember," one grandmother says. "But she remembered everyone who was at her party and a lot of the things that different family members said and did."

The Evolution of a Tradition

Traditions are not always permanent. Over time it is not uncommon for family traditions to change—not so much in the essence of the tradition but in the way the tradition is carried out.

Yolanda Sosa discovered this when her children started having families of their own. "We always made tamales at Christmastime," she explains. "I would tell my kids to reserve the date. They would all gather around to help. Then they started getting married and having children. Pretty soon all of them started picking up the tradition and making tamales with their own families. Now I go to their houses and help them."

Likewise, the family tradition of getting together on Christmas Eve may be the same, but it might not always be at the same house. Or your family might give up using your hand-painted Christmas china on Christmas Day and opt for dishes that can go into the dishwasher. In many families, adults cut back on gift giving and instead share photos or recipes.

One grandmother told everyone in the family that she didn't want any more gifts; instead, she asked them to say a Rosary for her. Other grandparents have resurrected the idea of spiritual bouquets, where a grandchild promises to say a certain number of Our Fathers or Hail Marys as a gift for someone in the family.

Being Flexible

Traditions don't have to be celebrated on the same day every year. Sometimes you need to be flexible.

"We celebrate the holidays when we can—not necessarily on the day," explains Veronica Cavan, who has three adult children and five grandchildren. "One year we celebrated Christmas on the day after Thanksgiving because we were all together. We put up the tree in the morning, and we exchanged gifts. We try not to put our children and our grandchildren in difficult positions. We try to make it easy, because they are already being pulled in a lot of different directions."

Sometimes new traditions arise out of changing circumstances. Gary and Kay Aitchison recall how a new tradition began in their family. "The year our first grandchild was born, they couldn't get home on Christmas Day," Kay explains. "So we had a grab-bag gift exchange with funny gifts for the rest of the family on Christmas Day. Everyone drew a number, and as each number was called, the person chose a gift and opened it. Someone else could steal a gift at their turn, and then the person whose gift was stolen could choose again. We exchanged our real presents when the whole family got together a few days later. The next year someone said, 'Aren't we going to do the grab bags?' Now it goes on every year. The night before our big family celebration, we have the grab-bag thing with goofy gifts. It has become a tradition."

Building Relationships

Christmas and Easter probably have the most family traditions associated with them, but it is important to remember that any recurring event can reinforce what it means to be a family. Birthdays, anniversaries, reunions, family picnics, and even fireworks on the Fourth of July can become part of a family's treasure trove of traditions.

Joe and Rose Mary Buscaglia have three married children and ten grandchildren. They get together every Sunday for dinner. "No matter how large or small a family or what nationality, family traditions are extremely important," Rose Mary says. "Through those traditions, we are teaching our children, whether we realize it or not, and we are also showing them the importance of being in relationship with one another. If you don't know what good relationships are, how can you have a relationship with God?"

The Myth of the Perfect Family

The problem with the notion of the perfect family—whether it's yours or someone else's—is that it is simply not true. As Catholics, we know that only God is perfect. Every human being has faults, weaknesses, and failings. Not even the greatest saints, who led extraordinary lives of holiness, were perfect. They all made mistakes.

It may be tempting to compare your family to other families, but it only leads to trouble. If you see your family as deficient, it stirs up feelings of jealousy. If you see your family as superior, it fuels a false sense of pride. It's a good idea to remind yourself that we are all children of a loving God who has given each of us unique gifts and talents. If you find yourself comparing your family to another family, you can stop yourself by offering a prayer for the other family.

The best way to keep everything in perspective is to thank God for all the good things that he has bestowed on you and on your family members and to trust that God will carry you through the difficult times. Your family may not be perfect, but you can count on God's grace to help you in every way.

> Dear families, you know very well that the true joy which we experience in the family is not superficial; it does not come from material objects, from the fact that everything seems to be going well. . . . True joy comes from a profound harmony between persons, something which we all feel in our hearts and which makes us experience the beauty of togetherness, of mutual support along life's journey. But the basis of this feeling of deep joy is the presence of God, the presence of God in the family and his love, which is welcoming, merciful, and respectful towards all.
> —Pope Francis, Homily, October 27, 2013

Questions for Reflection

1. What traditions does your family observe?

2. Have you ever had to modify an existing tradition or start a new tradition?

3. In what ways do you incorporate your Catholic faith into family traditions?

Grandparent Prayer

Gracious and loving God, guide me as I pass along the important traditions in our family. At the same time, Lord, keep me flexible enough to change or adapt traditions when the needs of our family change. Most of all, help me to instill in all our family gatherings a sense of gratitude to you for all the ways you have made yourself known to us. Amen.

—Chapter 21—

Family History

From the time she was a little girl, Kay Aitchison was captivated by family stories. As a grandmother, she makes it a point to pass the stories along.

"We need to know where we came from in order to know where we are going," she says. "It's a foundation. When you look back, past generations dealt with some really difficult things, and it is good for all of us to know about this—but especially children in the twenty-first century, as they get further away from those earlier times. I try to look for opportune moments when I can tell them about certain people in the family and where they came from."

When her grandchildren are young, Kay offers bits and pieces of information about people, places, and things. For their high school graduation, she gives them a bound copy of the family history. Her efforts are bearing fruit.

"One of my granddaughters interviewed me for a college project," Kay recalls. "She wanted to know what it was like for me growing up on a farm in Iowa. We had electricity, but we didn't have indoor plumbing. We walked to a country school."

Before visiting New York City, two other granddaughters wanted information on where their ancestors lived when they first came to this country.

"The history of a family is passed on in the telling of its stories," Kay says. "The richest families are those in which the stories have been incorporated into the spirit of the family."

Telling Family Stories

Kim Doyle has started to compile family history books for her children and grandchildren. "I went to the cemetery where my grandparents are buried, took pictures, and wrote down directions on how to get there. I put their pictures in the book. I'm sharing stories about them and what it was like for them growing up."

When you share family stories, you help your grandchildren put their lives in historical perspective. Storytelling also hones listening skills and activates a child's imagination. Whether the stories are happy, sad, funny, or too outlandish to be true, they form an invisible web that binds the family together.

One grandmother teaches her granddaughters how to sing a family lullaby that has been passed down through six generations. You can also share family sayings and bits of wisdom from previous generations. "My grandmother always said, 'God bless you and save you and keep you from harm,'" one grandmother recalls. "I find myself saying the same thing to my grandchildren."

Not everyone can share stories of ancestors from the 1800s. It doesn't matter. Children love to hear stories about their parents, aunts, and uncles. They delight in the exploits of family pets, descriptions of childhood games, recollections from birthday parties and family vacations, and the drama of daily life in the "olden days"—which may be only twenty years ago. Remember, our grandchildren never knew life without computers, cell phones, and color television.

With young children, you can keep your family history alive throughout the year with photo albums and scrapbooks. As children get older, you can help them make a family tree with names, dates of birth, marriages, and deaths. Encourage teens to create a video of family members, and then transcribe the stories into a family memory book.

Grandchildren of all ages like to hear stories about their own birth and early childhood. "I tell my grandchildren, 'I remember the day you were born!'" one grandfather says. "I tell them what I was doing that day and what the weather was like. I tell them how tiny they were and how careful I was the first time I got to hold them."

Sharing Faith Stories

Stories about sacramental moments in the family—baptisms, First Communions, confirmations, weddings, funerals, and even going to Mass as a family on Sundays and holy days—are important because they help children put their Catholic faith into a family context. These kinds of stories illustrate the important role that faith has played in the lives of family members during good times, bad times, and ordinary times. Through the stories, your grandchildren become witnesses to how family members embraced a moral code and how they cared for other people. Most important of all, they experience through stories the many ways God worked in the lives of different family members and how God's grace continues to support and sustain your family.

"Grandparents are a family's memory," Pope Francis says. "They are the ones who gave us the faith; they passed the faith on to us" (Address, September 26, 2015).

It takes some effort to keep children connected to the family, especially when extended family members are scattered all over the county. But the time and effort grandparents put into preserving family stories will reap benefits, particularly when grandchildren begin passing along stories about their own childhood to the next generation.

How to Get Started

Here are some creative ways that grandparents can share family stories with their grandchildren:

- Make a chart to help your grandchildren see where they fit in the family.

- Create a "Who's Who" of your family, with stories about different family members and how they are related.

- Save old family photos on a disk, and give copies to each family member.

- Take your grandchildren to visit the place where you grew up, your parish church, and the schools you attended.

- Share stories of what life was like when you were a child, what your parents and grandparents were like, what their occupations were, and how you spent your time as a family.

> The lack of historical memory is a serious shortcoming in our society. A mentality that can only say, "Then was then, now is now," is ultimately immature. Knowing and judging past events is the only way to build a meaningful future. Memory is necessary for growth.
> —Pope Francis, *Amoris Laetitia*, 193

Questions for Reflection

1. In what ways do you share your family stories with your grandchildren?

2. How is the Catholic faith part of your family history?

3. In what ways did your grandparents pass the Catholic faith on to you?

Grandparent Prayer

Lord, give me the wisdom to see the goodness in my family history, the patience to preserve our family memories, the understanding of how to pass this heritage on to my children, and the joy of knowing that your love binds all of this together. Amen.

Chapter 22

Family Fun

Barb Felix got an unexpected call from her grandson during the summer after his high school graduation. He wanted to join Barb and her husband, Fred, on their Vermont vacation. Barb and Fred were elated, and they even told their grandson he could bring his girlfriend, on the condition that she would sleep in the guest room and he would sleep on the living room couch.

The boy's father was surprised. "Why would they want to go on vacation with you and Dad?" he asked Barb.

"Because we're fun!" she replied.

Grandparents are fun, partly because they have lived long enough to know the kinds of things that kids love to do, and partly because they don't carry any responsibility for childrearing. Most grandparents have grown beyond the point where they care what other people think. They can be silly. They can sing songs. They can laugh at corny jokes. They can love, support, and have fun with their grandchildren without any strings attached. Even when grandparents are not physically capable of doing everything their grandchildren do, they can cheer from the sidelines.

Having Fun

Most grandparents know that fun doesn't have to be anything elaborate or expensive. Grandkids love simple activities such as feeding ducks, throwing stones in a creek, picking apples, flying a kite, eating a picnic lunch, and going to a beach.

When asked what kind of fun activities they like to do with grandchildren, the grandparent responses were wide-ranging:

- playing cards and board games
- drawing with chalk outside
- reading books
- building towers with blocks and knocking them down
- playing on the floor with the young ones
- doing arts and crafts
- building train sets
- having sleepovers
- cooking and baking
- playing dress-up
- going for a walk
- eating ice cream
- going to the park or the playground

The kinds of fun grandparents have with grandchildren are unique to each family. When Barb Wyse's three grandsons were little, they loved going to playgrounds. So Barb decided that her car would automatically stop at all playgrounds. "If we drove by a playground, we would stop and play for a while. Then we would get back in the car and do what we had to do. My grandsons are all young adults now, but they still talk about it. It was a lot of fun!"

When the grandchildren of Peter and Marianna Konieczny were little, Peter built a jungle gym for them. "Play with them. Joke with them. Have a sense of humor," he suggests.

Marianna agrees. "We always played together," she says. "We took them to parks and for pony rides. In the winter, we would play with snowballs. We created a skiing mountain, and they loved that. Being together is the most beautiful part."

One-on-One Time

It's fun to have the whole gang together, but there are also advantages to one-on-one time—which often starts with fun and evolves into more meaningful interactions and problem solving.

Joni Seith remembers the day she was giving her grandson an art lesson. He told Joni that he wasn't allowed to have a treat because he hadn't been good at Mass that morning. "I was talking at Mass, and I wasn't supposed to," he admitted. When Joni asked why, he told her that he was afraid he would forget what he wanted to ask Mommy, so he kept bothering her. Joni suggested that he take a little pad to Mass and draw pictures or write words to remind him of what he wanted to tell Mommy after Mass. "I'll be writing the whole time!" he told her.

Kay Aitchison agrees that individual interaction is important. "When they get to be young teenagers, they come and help with chores, and you have time for one-on-one," she says. "You get to know them in another way. If you can say the right things, it opens a lot of discussion possibilities."

Enjoying Every Moment

Michael and Sally Suchyna have seventeen grandchildren, and they enjoy watching them play soccer, basketball, hockey, and lacrosse; run track; and do gymnastics. They attend their grandchildren's concerts, plays, and dance recitals. "Over a year, we attend probably 150 to 200 of these events," Mike notes.

For the last twenty years, the Suchyna family has also taken a weeklong summer vacation at a lake house, along with some of their children and grandchildren. But Mike says it's not necessary to go away. Being together at home is wonderful too. "The Florida family usually comes up in the summer for two weeks, and we all have a great time when we get together with them," he explains. "We enjoy every moment."

Diane Germain agrees. She is the grandmother of six. "The best thing about being a grandparent is everything!" she says. "My grandchildren have taught me how to live life to the full and to live in the moment. They are my purest joy."

Faith and Fun

One of the best things about being Catholic is how much fun it can be to celebrate feast days and other special times. Here are some ideas on how grandparents can incorporate faith and fun with grandchildren of all ages:

- Celebrate saints. Let your children select favorite saints, read saints' stories, make saint costumes, and have your own saints parade.

- Play Christmas. Buy an unbreakable nativity set that your grandchildren can play with all year round. It will reinforce in their minds the true meaning of the season.

- Make rosaries with colored beads. Your grandchildren can give the rosaries to family members as gifts. Or donate the rosaries to the missions.

- Put on a play. Select a favorite Bible story, and let your grandchildren act it out. Letting stories come alive makes them more real.

- Make a Mass kit so your grandchildren can play Mass. You'll need a small box to use as an altar, a cloth to cover the box, a plastic cup, a small plate, a crucifix, and some candy wafers for "Communion." Some priests will tell you the seeds of their vocations were planted as they played Mass as children.

- Draw your guardian angels. Trace your grandchild on large paper, and let them draw wings and a halo on the image. Cut out the angel, and let your grandchild decorate with crayons.

- Play Catholic charades. Use songs, names of saints, Catholic phrases, and Bible stories. Your grandkids will love acting out the words and guessing the answers.

- Make Catholic cakes on feast days and other special occasions, decorating them with a cross, the initials of a saint, or some other symbol.

It is a joy and a great consolation to bring delight to others, to see them enjoying themselves.

Pope Francis, *Amoris Laetitia*, 129

Questions for Reflection

1. How do you have fun with your grandchildren?

2. How do you incorporate your Catholic faith into fun activities?

3. What advice would you give to other grandparents about having fun?

Grandparent Prayer

Dear Jesus, thank you for the gift of my grandchildren. Give me the strength to keep up with them! Give me patience. Protect me from irritability. Fill me with joy. Help me be the kind of grandparent that my grandchildren want to have fun with. Amen.

—Chapter 23—

Serving Others

*E*very year for the past twenty years, Marilyn Henry has been going on a mission trip to Guatemala with a Catholic lay missionary group called Sending Out Servants. When Marilyn's oldest granddaughter graduated from high school, Marilyn invited her to come along. They spent a week making home visits, helping with vacation Bible school, and sharing the faith with teens and adults. The trip made a big impression on Marilyn's granddaughter. Afterward she said, "When I was there, I don't think I appreciated it as much as I should have, but I think about it every day now."

Marilyn will soon have two grandchildren graduating from high school—a grandson and a granddaughter—and she plans to take both of them on mission with her.

Catholic social teaching and service to the poor are important to Marilyn and her husband, Ken, who is a deacon in their parish. Every summer, when all her grandchildren are together, Marilyn lets each draw a name of one of their cousins. Then Marilyn gives each grandchild ten dollars and takes them to a dollar store. They use half of the money to buy a gift for one of their cousins. With the other half, they buy a gift that they drop off at church for someone in need. "They have fun," Marilyn says, but more important, they learn about putting the needs of others ahead of their own.

The Call to Serve

As Catholics, we are called to serve the needs of the poor, the sick, and the most vulnerable members of our society. We know that we meet Christ when we help others, because Jesus told us that when we do something for the least of our brothers and sisters, we do it for him. "I was hungry and you gave me food, I was thirsty and you gave me drink, I was a stranger and you welcomed me, I was naked and you clothed me, I was sick and you visited me, I was in prison and you came to me" (Matthew 25:35-36).

When your grandchildren see you volunteer your time, donate money, and share what you have with people in need, they begin to understand that service is an important element of the Catholic faith. Young grandchildren will be happy to tag along in whatever you do. With older grandchildren, you can open a discussion about what areas of service they might find interesting or meaningful. You may be surprised at how social issues really matter to your grandchildren.

How Can We Help?

Donna Kaiser asks her grandchildren to help make cards and paper flowers for cancer patients. "But the thing they love to do most is go with me and my therapy dog to the nursing home!" she says.

Kim Doyle was brainstorming ideas for a service project with members of the grandparent group in her parish. One of the women mentioned that she had done a sandwich-making project in her home with her grandchildren the year before. The group decided to try it at the parish.

"We had twenty-five grandchildren and six grandparents," Kim recalls. "We assembled three hundred sandwiches for homeless shelters. We did that in thirty minutes, and afterward we went into the church for a visit with Jesus. We said a little prayer. Then we had a snack and went home."

Helping grandchildren put their faith in action has added benefits for grandparents. It gives you something meaningful to do with your grandchildren. It gives you something important to talk about. It helps you pass on an important element of our Catholic faith. And last but not least, it's fun!

Some Service Ideas

Here are some ideas for helping your grandchildren put their faith into action:

- Bring a bouquet of flowers to a nursing home.

- Deliver a bag of groceries to a local soup kitchen.

- Volunteer to sort canned goods at a local food pantry.

- Make chicken soup for a friend or family member who is sick.

- Offer to cut grass, rake leaves, shovel snow, or help an elderly neighbor with a home-improvement project.

- Let your grandchildren help you clean your basement, your attic, your closets, and your cupboards. Donate gently used items to a local charity.

- Plan a family project that will help the whole family appreciate and protect God's creation. It could be something as simple as growing seeds, planting a garden, or expanding your efforts to recycle and reuse.

- Invite your grandchildren to help you with a parish service project.

- Shop garage sales with your grandchildren to find toys that you can fix up and donate to a refugee center.

- Create a caring-and-sharing box in your home, where your grandchildren can place clothing, toys, coins, or other possessions that they want to share with people who are less fortunate. This will help them appreciate the fact that everything they have is a gift from God that is meant to be shared with others.

> As Christians, we have an additional reason to love and serve the poor; for in them we see the face and the flesh of Christ, who made himself poor so as to enrich us with his poverty (cf. 2 Corinthians 8:9).
> —Pope Francis, Address, July 11, 2015.

Questions for Reflection

1. How do you incorporate service into the practice of your Catholic faith?

2. In what ways have you introduced your grandchildren to the importance of serving others?

3. When have you recognized the presence of Christ in another person who was suffering?

Grandparent Prayer

Lord Jesus, at the Last Supper you washed the feet of the apostles as an example of how your followers are called to serve one another. Guide me as I encourage my grandchildren to reach out to people in need. Open their eyes so they can see the plight of the poor. Open their ears so they can heart the cries of the suffering. Open their hearts so they can respond in generosity and love. Amen.

Chapter 24

Family Dynamics

When Jack and Janet Mulvey were married in 1998, Jack had one grandchild and Janet had none. Today they have ten. "The first four were mine, and the last six were hers," Jack explains. "But they are all OURS. The kids don't know any different."

Most of Jack and Janet's grandchildren were born into their blended family. Jack's grandson was too young at the time of their marriage to remember any other family structure. It is more difficult to blend grandchildren who are old enough to know what life was like before Grandma or Grandpa remarried.

Nancy Allaire-Donohue's second husband is now deceased, but she remembers how challenging it was to blend her twenty-seven grandchildren with his five grandchildren. "If I had to give advice to someone going into a second marriage, it is to make them more aware of this one sentence: you are marrying the man or woman, but you are also marrying the family. So look at the family very carefully. You are taking on the other person's children and grandchildren."

Blended Families

There are no fast rules on how to blend a family. Here are some suggestions that might make things go more smoothly:

- No favoritism. Most stepgrandparents will secretly admit that while they love all their grandchildren, their biological grandchildren hold a special place in their hearts. The key to success, however, is not to show any preference for one over another.

- Go slowly. Don't expect your stepgrandchildren to instantly love you. Building relationships takes time. Look for things that you admire in each child. Allow new grandchildren to grow in their appreciation of you.

- Don't demand that everyone call you by the same name. Your stepgrandchildren might not want to call you Grandma or Grandpa. Let them decide what to call you.

- Try to get to know each child as an individual—their likes, dislikes, gifts, and talents.

- Don't try to force grandchildren into giving you hugs or kisses. Signs of affection should be spontaneous as a relationship develops.

- Be generous with your time.

- Make sure gifts and financial contributions are equal.

- Don't take sides in quarrels among stepgrandchildren and their parents. Their anger and resentment will often fall on you.

Blended families aren't the only family dynamic that impacts grandparents. Here are several other situations that can arise in families:

Adoption

Bob and Chris Gill have two adopted granddaughters from Guatemala. "We opened our arms to them," Chris recalls. "At first my daughter was concerned because the girls are dark skinned. She was afraid we might be prejudiced. But they are just the same as the other kids. They just blend in."

The Gills' adopted grandchildren were infants when they came into the family; that is not always the case. Today's adoptions might involve older children or special-needs children. Much of the advice offered on the previous pages for blended families will apply to grandparents of adopted children.

It is especially important that adopted grandchildren be treated equally. Without thinking, one grandmother gave copies of the family history to everyone in the family except her adopted grandchild. "You wouldn't want this because it really isn't your family," she said. The parents were angry, the child was hurt, and the grandmother realized afterward what a terrible mistake she had made.

Perhaps the best advice for grandparents of adopted children is to constantly strive for inclusion. Be careful what you say. If you inadvertently say or do something that your child or your adopted grandchild finds offensive, apologize immediately. Your adopted grandchild is a gift from God. He or she just came into your family in a different way.

Interfaith Marriages

Suzanne DeGraffenreid is a Catholic. Her husband is Presbyterian. Her grandchildren are being raised as evangelicals. "I walk a fine line," she admits. She doesn't push her Catholic beliefs on anyone, but she doesn't suppress her faith either. She understands that the keys to successful interfaith relationships are mutual respect and acceptance. If you are in a family with multiple faith experiences, here are some additional things to consider:

- Learn as much as you can about the faith of your grandchildren.

- Be supportive of their faith lives and experiences.

- Don't ever denigrate their religion.

- Participate in their religious milestones whenever you are invited.

- Be authentic in living your own faith.

- Answer questions about your faith honestly but only when asked.

- Don't try to convert them to the Catholic faith.

Nontraditional Families

Increasingly, grandparents find themselves navigating through nontraditional family relationships. In your family, you may have grandchildren living with Mom, grandchildren living with Dad, grandchildren living with parents in second marriages, grandchildren living with gay parents, grandchildren who have announced that they are gay, or grandchildren cohabitating with a boyfriend or a girlfriend.

"It's not the way I was raised," one grandfather lamented.

But nontraditional families are a reality that we face in our society today. "One of my girlfriends called me a few years ago with some hard news," a grandmother recalled. "Her daughter was pregnant and not married. My first reaction was 'Welcome to the grandparent club. Thank God she is going to have the baby. Life isn't always the way we've planned. But you are going to be a grandma, and that is wonderful!'"

"My friend really appreciated that. The baby was born a few months later, and her daughter decided to keep the baby. It is working out really well, and they are loving it."

Maintaining the Relationship

Under some circumstances, grandparents might not find it easy to adapt. But even if you are totally opposed to the decisions your children or grandchildren make, don't sever the relationship.

There are two ways that families cut off ties with one another. The first is a swift, sharp ending to the relationship in a flash of anger. The second is a slower process that takes place in stages:

- In the first stage, there is a gradual distancing. It starts when people refuse to talk about the situation and gradually grow apart.

- In the second stage, both sides begin to talk to other family members and friends in an attempt to build their own army of support for their position.

- In the third stage, negativity casts a dark shadow over things, and people can no longer see anything positive about the person or the situation.

- In the final stage, one or both sides have accumulated enough emotional energy to justify ending the relationship.

Severing a relationship is unhealthy, emotionally and spiritually. Try to remember that it is not the structure of the family that matters in terms of your relationships with your children and grandchildren. What matters is that we are called to love one another.

"I have several grandchildren who are living with a boyfriend or a girlfriend," one grandmother admits. "I'd rather see them get married than be in situations that are not good. I don't agree with what they are doing, but I still love them. I don't preach to them, but they know how I feel. It's the culture of the day."

How to Detach with Love

When faced with deep disappointment over the choices a family member makes in life, the best approach is to detach with love. Detachment is not cutting off the relationship. It is recognizing that you are not going to change this person and acknowledging that you don't know how the future will unfold. So you give it to God, with the hope that the Lord will take care of it. This approach leaves the door open, so that you can continue to love the person even if you disagree with what he or she is doing.

The strength of the family "lies in its capacity to love and to teach how to love. For all a family's problems, it can always grow, beginning with love."
—Pope Francis, *Amoris Laetitia*, 53, quoting Synod of Bishops, 2015, *Relatio Finalis*, 10

Questions for Reflection

1. What are some of the dynamics that impact your family?

2. In what ways do you deal with your disappointment involving family members?

3. How do you support your grandchildren in challenging family situations?

Grandparent Prayer

Lord, I struggle sometimes with my family dynamics. It's not always easy to be a grandparent. Help me to be non-judgmental. Help me to accept family situations that are out of my control. Teach me to love unconditionally and to be merciful as you are merciful. Amen.

Chapter 25

Away from the Catholic Faith

In today's world, it is not uncommon for children and grand-children to adopt completely different beliefs about God and attitudes toward religion from those of their parents and grand-parents. Half of young adults who were raised Catholic no longer identify themselves as Catholic. Some join a different church. Some remain Catholic but stop going to Mass. Some claim to be spiritual but not religious. Some reject all religion.

Traditionally, faith was part of the history, culture, and values that families passed from one generation to another. For example, families that are Irish, Polish, Italian, or Hispanic are generally assumed to be Catholic. For some grandparents, rejection of the Catholic faith by family members feels like rejection of an important element in the family.

"I can tell you about a whole bunch of people whose grand-children are away from the Church," one grandmother said. "These families put their hearts and souls into raising their kids Catholic, and they just don't understand how things turned out this way."

What Happened?

The reasons people give for no longer practicing their Catho-lic faith are varied, encompassing everything from "Church is boring" and "We're too busy" to lost faith, painful memories, and the hypocrisy of believers. Our increasingly secular culture has had an impact in marginalizing religious beliefs. Interfaith marriage is another factor, as well as lifestyle choices that are not in line with Catholic teaching.

"I have two sets of friends whose children married someone Jewish," one grandmother said. "In one family, the grandchildren are being raised Jewish. In the other family, the grandchildren are being raised Catholic, but they also celebrate Jewish holidays. There are all sorts of different things going on."

The strong emotional support offered in some nondenominational churches tends to draw in people after a death in the family, a divorce, or some other traumatic event. Some people are attracted by the family-oriented activities in some Protestant churches or the emphasis on a personal relationship with Jesus or a greater emphasis on Scripture. Sometimes people just drift away from their Catholic faith.

In the final analysis, there is often no good explanation why some family members maintain a strong connection to the Catholic faith and others do not.

Whose Fault Is It?

"In my years as a pastor, I have seen so many people in tears over this," says Fr. James Mallon, host of the *Grandparents* series. "They ask, 'Was it my fault? Did I do enough?'"

If parents raise their children in a Catholic home and practice their faith, they fulfill their responsibility, and they cannot blame themselves for a decision that their adult child makes. But what if the parents did not do everything they could to raise their children in the Catholic faith?

"There will always be sins of omission or commission," says Fr. Mallon, "but you have to repent, and you need to move on. If you are burdened by guilt, you are not going to be free to be used by God to reach your children or your grandchildren. You have to live in the grace of God and move on."

Fr. Mallon also points out that parents are not the only influence in their children's faith development. They may bear some responsibility for their adult children's failure to practice their faith, but a large portion of responsibility might lie elsewhere.

"A lot of these grandparents were taught the faith by their parents, and they did what their parents did in terms of passing on the faith to their own children," Fr. Mallon explains. "But it didn't work because of the huge cultural shift in the past fifty years, and it is not their fault that their children left the Church."[11]

So whose fault is it? Only God can search people's hearts and answer that question. Sometimes we just have to accept the decisions that other people make.

Jesus offered us a remarkable example of this kind of acceptance when the rich young man walked away from him (Mark 10:17-22). Jesus didn't try to talk the young man into staying. Jesus didn't ask himself, "What could I have done to prevent this?" Jesus didn't see himself as a failure. Jesus was sad, but he respected the young man's free will. Jesus looked at the young man with love and allowed him to walk away.

Letting Go with Love

"The one thing I always say to people is that God loves these children more than you do," says Kim Doyle, who coordinates the grandparent ministry at her parish. "We've had speakers come to our group who said, 'Pray for your grandchildren, and trust that God wants them home more than you do. You may not see it in your lifetime, but you will be together in heaven.'"

Kim keeps a picture of Jesus holding a lost lamb—it gives her comfort and strength. "It's hard to believe that someone can love your grandchild more than you do," she says, "but God does. So put them into his hands."

The Example of St. Monica

St. Monica experienced great anguish over her pagan husband, who had a violent temper, and her son Augustine, whose intellectual snobbery and pursuit of his own pleasure led him into an immoral lifestyle. She prayed that her husband and her son would one day embrace the truth of Christianity.

According to Augustine's *Confessions*, written after his conversion, Monica begged a local bishop to speak with her son. The bishop refused, advising her to leave Augustine alone for a while and concentrate on praying for him. When Monica continued to plead with the bishop, he told her, "Go your way; it cannot be that the son of these tears should perish." Monica accepted his words as "a voice from heaven."[12]

Eventually, Monica's husband and Augustine were baptized. Their conversions are attributed to St. Monica's prayers and the example of her virtuous life. St. Augustine went on to become a priest, bishop, and doctor of the Church. August 27 is St. Monica's feast day; August 28 is St. Augustine's.

Patience takes root when I recognize that other people also have a right to live in this world, just as they are. It does not matter if they hold me back, if they unsettle my plans, or annoy me by the way they act or think, or if they are not everything I want them to be. Love always has an aspect of deep compassion that leads to accepting the other person as part of this world, even when he or she acts differently than I would like.

—Pope Francis, *Amoris Laetitia*, 92

Questions for Reflection

1. Who are the people in your family no longer practicing their Catholic faith?

2. How do you maintain positive relationships with these family members?

3. How have you let go of painful feelings associated with loved ones who have strayed from Catholicism?

Grandparent Prayer

Gracious and loving God, you know the pain I feel because of family members who no longer practice their Catholic faith. Help me to love as you love. Keep me from being judgmental. Give me the wisdom to know when to speak and what to say. Give me patience to bear silently the sorrow I feel. Allow your Holy Spirit to work through me so that my faith can become a positive example in their lives. Amen.

Chapter 26

When Grandparents Baptize

*F*or Catholic grandparents, there is great joy in witnessing the baptism of a grandchild. Even though a baby is too young to understand, grandparents know that the Sacrament of Baptism makes this child a participant in the life of Christ.

But what happens when parents refuse to have their children baptized?

"My grandchildren are not being raised in any religion because my son is an adamant atheist," one grandparent said. "So I baptized all of my grandchildren with holy water."

Stories abound of worried grandparents who baptize grandchildren in the bathtub, in the kitchen sink, or with a garden hose. While their intentions may be good, there are serious moral and spiritual questions about their actions.

What the Church Teaches

As harsh as this may sound, baptizing a grandchild without the parents' permission is against the teaching of the Catholic Church. According to canon law, "For an infant to be baptized lawfully, it is required that the parents, or at least one of them, or the person who lawfully holds their place, give their consent" (Canon, 868).

The *Catechism of the Catholic Church* tells us that the Sacrament of Baptism serves as the foundation of the Christian life. It washes away sin, incorporates the newly baptized person into the body of Christ, and gives that person a new life in the Spirit. "Baptism is the sacrament of faith. But faith needs the community of believers" (CCC 1253; cf. Mark 16:16).

Since infants and children are not capable of giving their consent for baptism, the parents act on the child's behalf and accept the responsibility to nurture the child's faith. As part of the Rite of Baptism, the parents express their desire that the child be baptized, and the priest recognizes that the parents are the child's first teachers. In this sense, baptism is only a beginning step in the faith life of the child.

As the child grows older, it is the parents' duty to help their child encounter Christ in Scripture, the sacraments, prayer, faith sharing, service to others, and worship in a parish community. If there is no hope of this happening, then the Catholic Church insists that the baptism not take place. The only exception to this rule is if a child is in imminent danger of death.

Emergency Baptisms

"I was baptized by my mother because they thought I was going to die," explains Fr. James Mallon, host of the *Grandparents* series. "The baptism that my mother performed was a valid baptism. The Church teaches that a layperson can baptize in cases of emergency."

But Fr. Mallon does not approve of grandparents baptizing grandchildren against the parents' wishes. He has two nephews who are not baptized. "Neither of my sisters goes to church," he explains. "I have had this discussion about baptism with my parents and other family members. If a grandparent baptizes, it might be valid, but what does that mean if it bears no fruit? Yes, there will be an imprinting and configuration to Christ. But it is far removed from the original meaning of baptism, which was to repent, to believe, and then to be baptized into the life of Christ and the Church. I think grandparents need to be mindful of that."

Fear of Original Sin

Most grandparents who resort to baptizing admit that they act out of a desire to cleanse their grandchild of original sin. "Original sin is not actually a sin," Fr. Mallon explains. "Original sin is the natural human condition. Baptism does bring children into a state of grace until the age of reason, when they can say no to God and sin for the first time. But this understanding of baptism is a very thin sliver of what the sacrament is about.

"So when grandparents baptize, they have the original sin concept covered, but it becomes self-contradictory because there is no life for the child in the Church. The baptism is hidden and unknown. The parents are not aware of it. The child is not aware of it. It is a highly reduced understanding of what baptism really is."[13]

Fear of Limbo

Related to this limited understanding of baptism is the fear many grandparents have that a child who dies without baptism will go to a place called limbo. Catholic teaching about limbo began after St. Augustine (354–430) taught that a soul could not enter heaven without baptism. Before long, questions arose as to what happens to babies who die before they receive the sacrament. In an attempt to reconcile God's infinite mercy with this teaching on baptism, theologians identified limbo as a place of natural happiness, like heaven, but without the presence of God.

In 2007, the International Theological Commission, which Pope St. John Paul II established to study the Church teaching on limbo, issued a document entitled "The Hope of Salvation for Infants Who Die without Being Baptized." In this document, the theologians concluded that there are "serious theological and liturgical grounds for hope that unbaptized infants who die will be saved and enjoy the beatific vision." They placed their trust in "the God of mercy and love who has been revealed to us in Christ." They expressed "strong grounds for hope" that God will save infants who die without baptism. Pope Benedict XVI authorized the publication of the document and its conclusions.

What Grandparents Can and Cannot Do

Most priests will tell you that baptizing a child without the parents' knowledge or consent is dishonest and a betrayal of the parents' rights and responsibilities. There are stories of parents becoming so upset when they learned a grandparent had baptized their child that they obtained court orders barring the grandparent from any further contact with that child and any future children born into the family.

"I have four grandchildren who are not baptized, and it grieves my soul," one grandmother said. "None of my children go to church, and I pray for that as well. My daughter says they don't believe in organized religion, but she loves groups that help people, like Catholic Charities. I softly point out that unless religions are organized and spiritually directed, they can't do things like Catholic Charities or help anyone in need. I know God is at work in their lives and hearts, and all is in *his* time and not mine. I just wait and share what and when I can."

While waiting and praying is not always easy, it is the best approach. Sometimes it bears fruit.

"When my oldest grandchild was born, my son was not married to the baby's mother," another grandmother recalls. "He used to bring my granddaughter to our house on the weekends, and she spent a lot of time with us. I never baptized her. I just tried to incorporate her into my faith life and the faith of our family. When she was a young teenager, she asked if she could become a Catholic like the rest of our family."

Sometimes grandparents find other ways to intercede.

"My daughter wanted her kids baptized, but she admitted that she had no intention of going back to church herself," one grandmother explains. "We went with her to talk with our parish priest about baptizing her children. My husband and I assured the priest that we would do everything in our power to oversee our grandchildren's faith development, and he agreed to baptize our grandchildren under those conditions. My advice for grandparents in similar situations is to understand the true meaning of baptism and to keep the lines of communication open with the parents of your grandchild and with your parish priest."

Fr. Mallon suggests that instead of baptizing, concerned grandparents can bless their grandchild. "There is a Rite of Blessing, and there are parts in the rite for a layperson to bless. So it is all right to bless your grandchild. You can pray over your grandchild. You can lay hands on your grandchild. You can dedicate your grandchild to God. But don't baptize unless the child is in imminent danger of death."

Talking to Your Children about Baptism

Here are some simple tips for talking with your adult child about the baptism of his or her child:

- Start talking before the baby is born.

- Ask the prospective parents if they are planning to have the baby baptized.

- Be prepared to answer questions about the Sacrament of Baptism. If you don't know the answer to a question, promise to find out.

- Try to listen to what your adult child is saying without getting upset or passing judgment.

- Remember that words are the smallest part of communication. Your tone of voice, body language, and attitudes communicate more than words.

- Never, never, never raise your voice or lose your temper.

- If the decision is made not to baptize the baby, don't argue.

- You may not understand or approve, but try to accept whatever decision your adult child makes.

- Acknowledge that you have different opinions but that you still love one another.

Baptism is the sacrament on which our very faith is founded and which grafts us as a living member onto Christ and his Church.

—Pope Francis, Audience, January 8, 2014

Questions for Reflection

1. Did you open a discussion about the baptism of your grandchildren with your son or daughter? How did you begin?

2. In what ways are you coping with your son or daughter's refusal to have your grandchild baptized?

3. What advice would you offer to other grandparents in this situation?

Grandparent Prayer

Lord, you know how upset I am about my unbaptized grandchildren. Help me understand and accept my responsibility as a grandparent. Keep me from overstepping my bounds. Deepen my faith and trust in you. Strengthen my relationship with the parents of my grandchild. Teach me how to love as you love. Amen.

Chapter 27

Dealing with Death

When Charlie Donner was diagnosed with an aggressive form of lymphoma, his seven grandchildren were told right away that Grandpa was sick with something called cancer and that the doctors were trying to make him better.

"For the next five years, there were good times and there were tough times," his wife, Teri, recalls.

When Charlie was doing well, the Donners would invite their grandchildren for sleepovers, swimming, and trips to the zoo. When Charlie had a bone marrow transplant, the children came to the hospital to visit. "I think I know now that the cancer is all gone," one of the grandsons said.

But the cancer was not gone, and when doctors explained that there was nothing else they could do, the grandchildren were told that Charlie was going to die.

"They all had the opportunity to talk to him," Teri recalls. "He told them what good parents they had. He told them to help take care of me. It was good, because they knew him as a lively and fun person, and they had to know that this was how they were going to say good-bye."

After Charlie died, Teri encouraged her grandchildren to talk about their feelings. "The kids have a real sense of things," she explains. "I'll hear them say, 'Grandpa is in heaven.' We'll talk about how he is happy now and how he doesn't have any more pain. But it's not something that we dwell on."

Still, there is a profound sense of loss. One of Teri's granddaughters said, "It's like a piece of our puzzle is missing."

How Grandchildren Grieve

Children are deeply impacted by a death in the family. Whether they lose a parent, a sibling, a grandparent, an aunt, an uncle, or even a beloved family pet, children can experience the feelings of shock, anger, and sadness that adults feel. But they might not express their grief in the same way.

You might notice children acting out or becoming silent and withdrawn. They may have difficulty expressing their feelings. They may be afraid someone else is going to die. They may have questions about why God allowed this to happen. They may be frightened by the grief of other family members.

Young children might regress to thumb sucking, bed wetting, or whining. They might have nightmares or refuse to be left alone. Older children and teens might exhibit anger or moodiness. Schoolwork may suffer.

How Grandparents Can Help

Grandparents are often in a unique position to help grandchildren when someone in the family is terminally ill or has died. The key is to keep the lines of communication open. Encourage grieving grandchildren to speak freely and to ask as many questions as they want.

Peter and Marianna Konieczny say that it was "very, very difficult" when their grandson, Dominik Pettey, was killed in an automobile accident.

"Our grandchildren were very sad," Marianna recalls. "They were crying. We were all together. We tried to comfort them. We talked to them and explained to them that someday we will all go to heaven and meet each other. They could understand that.

"Now when we go to his grave, they kneel with us and they pray. They feel Dominik's presence and the mystery of God. It is very difficult, but prayer is helping us. Prayer is the essence, the core. Peace comes from the Holy Spirit when we pray. It comes from God, and it gives us strength."

Here are some suggestions on how grandparents can support their grandchildren in times of illness and death:

• Let your grandchildren express their feelings through words or drawings.

• Admit that you are also experiencing a range of emotions.

• Assure your grandchildren that the illness or death is not their fault.

• Encourage grandchildren to ask questions.

• Answer questions honestly. If there is no answer, say so.

• Allow grandchildren to cry.

• Help grandchildren create a memorial by putting together a scrapbook, writing a story, planting a tree, or finding some other way to remember the person who died.

• Pray together.

Explaining Heaven to Grandchildren

St. Augustine described heaven as "ineffable," which is another way of saying it is beyond words. So what do you say when your grandchildren ask questions about heaven? Here are some suggestions:

- If your grandchild asks where heaven is, reply that heaven is where people who have died go to be with God.

- If your grandchild asks what heaven is like, admit that no one knows until they go there but that Jesus promised that it would be a very special place.

- If your grandchild asks if people in heaven can see people on earth, explain that as Catholics, we believe that there is a connection between people in heaven and on earth. Encourage your child to ask loved ones in heaven to pray for them.

- If your grandchild asks if he or she can go to heaven, explain to your child that we don't go to heaven until all our work on earth is done, but someday we will all be together in heaven.

- If your grandchild asks something that you're unsure of, say, "I don't know. Let's figure out where we can get the answer to that question!"

The Preface of the Liturgy of the Dead puts it nicely: "Although the certainty of death saddens us, we are consoled by the promise of future immortality. For the

life of those who believe in you, Lord, is not ended but changed." Indeed, "our loved ones are not lost in the shades of nothingness; hope assures us that they are in the good strong hands of God."
—Pope Francis, *Amoris Laetitia*, 256, quoting the Liturgy of the Dead and General Audience of June 17, 2015

Questions for Reflection

1. Have you struggled with illness and death in your family? What were the circumstances?

2. How have you supported your grandchildren in their grief or observed other grandparents supporting their grandchildren?

3. What role does your Catholic faith play in the grieving process?

Grandparent Prayer

Lord, give me the wisdom and the courage that I will need in helping my grandchildren deal with illness and death in our family. Give me the words that will comfort them. Shower all of us with your love and your peace. Amen.

—*Chapter 28*—

Dealing with Divorce

"**M**y grandson was about eight years old when his parents decided to get divorced," one grandmother recalls. "I asked him how he was doing with everything that was going on."

"Well," he said, "what's so bad about divorce? We are still a family. We still love each other. We are just going to be sleeping in two different houses."

This grandmother was relieved. "By the time the decision was made to divorce, the parents had already been in counseling for over a year, and a lot of the details had been worked out. There weren't a lot of issues. The parents have joint custody, and it is very well organized."

It would be wonderful if all divorces were this amicable and if all children of divorce were as well adjusted. But that isn't the case.

The Pain of Divorce

In many ways, divorce is the death of a marriage, and everyone in the family must grieve that loss. Before you can help your grandchildren, you need to deal with your own feelings about the divorce. Start by giving yourself permission to grieve. You may struggle with sadness, anger, resentment, worry, or fear of what might happen in the future.

Divorce shatters the unrealistic image of being a perfect family. "I struggled with feelings of shame," one grandmother admitted. "This was the first divorce in our family. I didn't know how I was going to tell other family members and friends."

Keep in mind that feelings will ebb and flow. Talking to a priest, a spiritual director, a counselor, or a trusted friend can help you dissipate some of the raw energy inside you. Talking eases the pain and lessens the risk that you will say or do something that you will later regret.

Don't Take Sides

It is important to keep the lines of communication open with everyone. Assure both parents that you want the best for them and for your grandchildren. You may find yourself in a position in which one or both parents share their feelings with you. Resist the temptation to offer advice.

Don't fall into the trap of placing blame. Remember that there are many factors involved when a marriage ends in divorce. Even if you struggle with resentment, don't let it show. You may not be good friends with the other parent, but try to be gracious and respectful. The amount of contact you have with your grandchildren in the future will depend on your relationship with both parents as you all go through this crisis.

"I actually got along better with my daughter-in-law after the divorce," one grandparent acknowledged. "She still needed help running kids around to activities. I filled a need, and it worked out well for both of us."

Be a Port in the Storm

A 2009 Oxford University study of grandparent-adolescent relationships involved fifteen hundred grandchildren. Among other findings, it demonstrated that grandparents were an important source of emotional stability for grandchildren in families of divorce.[14] Assure your grandchildren of your love.

Reinforce the fact that both their parents love them. Let them know that the divorce is not their fault. Acknowledge that life is difficult now, but everything will get better eventually.

Depending on the ages of your grandchildren, they may or may not want to talk about what is happening. If they clam up, don't try to force a conversation. If they want to talk, be a compassionate listener.

It's okay to admit to your grandchildren that you feel sad about what is happening, but don't ever say anything negative about either parent. Be especially careful when answering their questions. Don't get into the details of the divorce. It's not up to you to let them know why their parents are getting a divorce or how their living arrangements might change. It's always best to refer them back to their parents.

"I've just dealt with a friend whose family was going through a divorce," one grandmother explains. "Grandparents have to be very supportive and a bit in the background. Grandchildren especially need love and support. The grandparents can be the stability for kids at that time in their lives."

Praying Through a Divorce

During a divorce, prayer is one of the most positive things you can do with your grandchild. Start by explaining that sometimes bad things happen in people's lives. Acknowledge that everybody has difficulties in life. Your family is not the only family that has gone through the pain of divorce. But God will help everyone in the family to get through it.

Don't ever suggest that children pray for their parents to get back together. Instead, encourage your grandchildren to pray that God will comfort their parents and give them strength.

Pray that God will take away the sadness. Pray that God will take away anger and feelings of resentment. Pray for all the members of your family. Remind your grandchildren to pray for themselves.

In families, there are difficulties, but those difficulties are resolved by love. Hatred doesn't resolve any difficulty. Divided hearts do not resolve difficulties. Only love is capable of resolving difficulty. Love is a celebration, love is joy, love is perseverance.

—Pope Francis, Address, September 26, 2015

Questions for Reflection

1. Have marital difficulties impacted your family? In what ways?

2. Did you maintain open lines of communication during this difficult time? What might you have done differently?

3. Were you able to serve as a support for your grandchildren?

Grandparent Prayer

Lord, my emotions are running wild as I try to help my grandchildren deal with their parents' divorce. Give me the strength to support them through this. Give me the wisdom to know what to say and what to do. Let them see that my love for them will never end. Amen.

Divorce Statistics for Catholics

According to the Center for Applied Research in the Apostolate at Georgetown University, an estimated 28 percent of American Catholic adults have divorced. This is lower than the overall divorce rate for Americans, but it still represents more than 11 million people.[15]

—*Chapter 29*—

Under One Roof

Dave and Michelle Wyse decided to build a house, but they needed a place to live in the interim. They asked Dave's mother if they and their three young children could move in with her.

"The twins were two, and Jeremy was six when they came to live with me," Barbara Wyse says. "They stayed for a year and a half, but it was never a problem."

Before they moved in, Dave, Michelle, and Barbara sat down and talked about details. "We set up what space they would have. They took care of their own groceries, and we split the utilities. We would eat each other's food, but they did their own grocery shopping so they knew they would have enough. Sometimes when I would cook, they would eat what I was eating if they were around. If not, we each did our own thing. At that time in my life, I was out most of the time."

Barbara was teaching full-time, and she was busy with after-school activities. Three nights a week, she had meetings at her parish. "Dave and Michelle did not assume that because I was here, I would automatically be willing to babysit," Barb recalls. "They were very careful to ask me. Sometimes when they went out with the kids, I would have the whole house to myself, which was nice every now and then."

A Growing Trend

It's not rare for grandparents to offer shelter to their children and grandchildren. Nearly eight million children live in homes where grandparents are present, and those numbers are expected to increase. Reasons range from financial issues and home remodeling to the death of parents, divorce, drug or alcohol addiction, teenage pregnancy, and incarceration.

Sometimes, as in Barbara's case, the living arrangements are temporary. In other families, the situation becomes permanent.

"My reflection is that it presents a unique challenge because the parent is still the parent, the grandparents are grandparents, and the children have to be respectful of the grandparents' spaces," explained one grandmother whose daughter and two grandchildren moved in with her. "The children still have to observe the rules of the household. So there is a constant tension."

Who Makes the Rules?

Rules are essential in order to maintain peaceful coexistence, and it is best if the adults can sit down and decide on discipline ahead of time, along with appropriate consequences for bad behavior.

"To be honest, my wife and I are doing most of the parenting," said one grandfather. "My son and daughter-in-law are not strong parents. So we set up the rules in our house, and the kids know that if they violate those rules, there will be consequences. It's a struggle because my son doesn't always agree with what we do. But it is important to have boundaries when you have grandchildren living with you."

Grandparents who have grandchildren living with them also stress the need to create a sense of family but, at the same time, maintain a sense of separateness. Grandparents, parents, and children need some separate space where they can retreat to be alone. There should be rules for the common areas of the home that place limits on television, music, and the use of electronics. It is also a good idea to set up a routine for meal-times, bedtimes, and household chores.

"There can be some flexibility," one grandmother says, "but having separate space is important for keeping the peace."

When Grandparents Raise Grandchildren

Grandparents who are raising their grandchildren face different problems. They become the sole custodians of their grandchildren, and the responsibility can weigh heavily on them. "It is very isolating to be a grandparent raising grandchildren, because you may not have peers doing the same thing," one grandmother observed. "You are stuck at home while your peers are out traveling and enjoying an empty nest, so finding a grandparent support system is essential."

Deb Dowd-Foley, a licensed social worker with Elder Services in Worcester, Massachusetts, agrees. "When the grandparents get into a support group, they realize they are not alone. They learn from each other."

Support groups help to dispel some of the self-doubt that grandparents may feel about whether they are capable of doing a good job raising grandchildren. "Some of these grandparents are still working," Dowd-Foley explains. "Many of the grandparents who are retired have health issues. All of these grandparents have to balance taking care of themselves and taking care of their grandchildren. They don't have the same energy level that a parent would have. Some of them are dealing with grandchildren who have mental health issues or autism or behavioral problems. When the biological parent is in and out of the picture, it can add to the stress. A lot of these grandparents are overwhelmed."

At one session for grandparents raising grandchildren, the group brought in a speaker who was a successful artist for children's book publishers. He was raised by his grandparents because his mother was a heroin addict. It was inspiring and reassuring for the grandparents to hear him speak, because he was so appreciative of everything his grandparents had done for him.

"There are many layers of concern when grandparents are raising grandchildren," Dowd-Foley says. "Finances, child care, discipline, giving up the role of being a grandparent, and taking on the responsibility of parenting are all part of it. These grandparents do amazing things to help their grandchildren."

On the Plus Side

While there are certainly challenges involved with living under one roof, there are also a lot of positive experiences that grandparents experience when grandchildren live with them. There is a sense of joy in being intimately involved in the lives of their grandchildren as they reach their various milestones. There is the satisfaction that comes when you can impart some of the wisdom you have acquired with age. There is the happiness of helping them solve a problem. There is the thrill of teaching them a skill that you have mastered. And there is the fun of just being together.

"Living together also puts us in a unique position to share our Catholic faith with our grandchildren," one grandparent says. "We have a rule that all children under eighteen have to go to church with us on Sunday morning. My daughter doesn't go, but the kids do. We enrolled them in religious education in our parish. We say prayers at bedtime and when we eat meals together. We really try hard to impart our faith. It has been worth it because our grandkids are strong in their Catholic faith."

Some Helpful Hints for Grandparents Living with Grandchildren

- Set up a routine for your household.
- Maintain contact with friends and other family members.
- Find a trusted person to talk with about your situation.
- Don't expect perfection in yourself or anyone else.
- Set aside some quiet time for yourself.
- Learn relaxation techniques.
- Don't neglect your health. Get regular checkups.
- Find some form of exercise that you can do regularly—even if it is just walking around the block.
- Don't give up your hobbies or other interests.
- Seek comfort in prayer and meditation.
- Join a grandparent support group or a faith-sharing group in your parish.
- If you feel that things are getting out of hand, seek help from a professional.

I pray for you and with you, and I ask God our Father to accompany you and to bless you, to fill you with his love and defend you on your way by granting you in abundance that strength which keeps us on our feet: that strength is hope, the hope that does not disappoint.

—Pope Francis, Address, July 9, 2015

Questions for Reflection

1. In what ways have you or someone you know experienced living with grandchildren?

2. What do you see as the greatest challenges to multiple generations living together?

3. How can you support and encourage family members or friends who are raising grandchildren?

Grandparent Prayer

Gracious and loving God, you know how difficult it is at times for all of us to live together. Instill in us deep respect for one another. Strengthen our family bond. Increase our love. Help us live together in peace and harmony. Amen.

Chapter 30

Support for Grandparents

Several years ago, Jolana Peard, a pastoral associate at St. Robert of Newminster Parish in Ada, Michigan, noticed that increasing numbers of grandparents were volunteering in religious education programs and vacation Bible school. When a co-worker showed Jolana a postcard advertising a grandparent camp at a local university, the idea for a Catholic grandparent camp at the parish was born.

"It is like a vacation Bible school but for grandparents and grandchildren ages eight to twelve," Jolana says. "We have between thirty and forty participants every year. We always pick a theme that has a family component to it, because we want the grandparents to not only do faith sharing but to share something about their lives."

The theme for the first year was the Jesse Tree, and Jolana used trees as a basis for the activities. In a segment called "The Apple Doesn't Fall Far from the Tree," the grandparents and grandchildren compared how they were alike and how they were different, starting with the color of their eyes and the color of their hair. "They also mapped their family tree," Jolana explains. "We had a map of the United States and a map of the world, so they could talk about where their families came from and where other family members live today."

When Noah's Ark was chosen as the theme, Jolana brought in live animals. For the Holy Family theme, participants talked about the fact that Jesus lived in a family and that he had grandparents too.

Each day there is a song, a game, and a snack that tie in with the theme. As a memento from the week, they might make a scrapbook, a memory box, or a photo frame containing a picture of themselves.

"The grandparents love it," Jolana says. "They like to share their faith and have fun doing it. I want the kids to have a good time too so that they have a good feeling about church."

Fred and Fran Gilhoran have been campers for four years. They say the best part is spending time with their grandchildren and "having nothing to do but show up!"

The Importance of Support

Crystal Crocker, who coordinates grandparent ministries in the Archdiocese of St. Paul and Minneapolis, witnessed an explosion of excitement and involvement after introducing grandparent workshops, parish support groups, and an annual grandparent conference that attracts hundreds of participants. She also established an advisory board, with grandparents who help identify the needs of grandparents in the archdiocese and how those needs can be met.

"Our secular society has been attacking the family from every aspect, and this is one of the first ways to bring the family back," she says. "When we first got started, some of the people I worked with would say, 'A grandparent ministry—how sweet!' But the fact of the matter is that it is quite strategic because grandparents are the second influencers to the grandchildren."

Crystal points out that grandparents are also easy to reach. "They are already in the pews. They want to come together. They want support. They have the time, the resources, the need, and a wealth of formation in their faith that they can share with their grandchildren."

Starting a Support Group

Several years ago, at the suggestion of her parish priest, Colette Byrne started a small discussion group for grandmothers in her home in Phoenix, Arizona. "The second year, the husbands were asking why they couldn't come, so we invited them," Colette explains. "Now we have five couples who meet on Monday mornings."

The group rotates houses. They have a sit-down breakfast, and afterward they pray a scriptural Rosary together, adding their intentions for their families and grandchildren. Then they read and discuss the Gospel passage from the Sunday before and share their reflections.

"It is interesting, because a few are from different parishes, and we share how the homily in each parish addressed the Gospel," Colette says. "We have developed close relationships with one another and have become great prayer partners. Whenever one of us has a family crisis, we text or call and know that we have ten people who will fervently pray for our intentions."

No Longer Alone

One of the greatest benefits of grandparent ministries and support groups is knowing that you are not alone.

"There are a lot of stresses in families," says Kim Doyle, who started a grandparent support group in her parish in Rosemount, Minnesota. "There are a lot of broken families. How can we help to heal that? The more people you get having a conversion, the more you are going to get someone saying, 'Hey, I've got that problem too.' Then those two grandparents form a friendship and a support system. It's interesting, because as my grandparent group has grown, some of the people who were reluctant to share the 'stuff' in their family are pouring it out now. It is so freeing. I can see the healing in them, and it has been such a blessing to witness."

Good Examples

When Fr. James Mallon agreed to produce the *Grandparents* series, his hope was to show grandparents how important they are in the lives of their grandchildren and the great potential grandparents have for passing along their faith. He filmed the series in Halifax, Nova Scotia.

"The young people we interviewed in the videos saw their grandparents going to Mass or reading Scripture or praying the Rosary," Fr. Mallon explains. "The grandparents took time to talk with their grandchildren about faith and answer their questions."

Kim Doyle used Fr. Mallon's videos with her grandparent support group. "Never in any of those videos did anyone say, 'My grandparents sat me down with a Bible and said this or that,'" Kim recalls. "It was all about watching the grandparents interact and how caring their grandparents were to their neighbors. They saw their grandmother go to Mass by herself. When she would come home, they would ask where she had gone, and it got them interested. They began to ask if they could go too."

Kim encouraged the members of her support group to apply what they were seeing on the videos to their own lives. It helped them recognize the many ways they were already living their faith.

"At some point, your grandchildren are going to ask you questions about the meaning of life, and when that time comes, speak and testify to Jesus," Fr. Mallon advises. "You may not see visible fruit in your own lifetime, but your ability to witness with your love and your joy will make a difference in the lives of your grandchildren."

Resources for Grandparent Support

Here is a handy list of resources for those who want to learn more about support for grandparents:

- **Archdiocese of St. Paul and Minneapolis Catholic Grandparent Ministry**

The Catholic Grandparent Ministry strives to build a community of support and healing for grandparents, to encourage them to live holy lives, and to equip them with the tools to build up their families and parishes in Christ. The website contains information on how to start a grandparent support group and offers links to other resources, including videos, books, workshops, study groups, conferences, organizations, and websites. Website: www.catholicgrandparenting.org

- **Catholic Grandparents Association**

The Catholic Grandparents Association is an international private Association of the Faithful with members and chapters in parishes worldwide. Its mission is to support grandparents in passing on the faith and keeping prayer at the heart of family life. The CGA website offers step-by-step instruction on how to become a member and/or start a chapter.

Catholic Grandparents Association
135 SE 5th Ave.
Delray Beach, Delray, FL 33483
Phone: 713-244-4217 or 888-510-5006
Website: www.catholicgrandparentsassociation.org

- *The Grand Adventure: A New Call to Grandparenting*

This six-session discussion program written by Deacon Gary and Kay Aitchison includes an opening prayer and Scripture reflection, a topic for discussion, and action ideas. *The Grand Adventure* can be used with a group of friends or in the development of a parish program for grandparents. To order the program or to download the first session for free, go to www. cfm.org/program_books. For additional information, contact

CFM USA National Office
PO Box 4779
Woodbridge, VA 22194-4779
Phone: 800-581-9824
E-mail: office@cfm.org
Website: www.cfm.org

- *Grandparents* with Fr. James Mallon

This EWTN video series features Fr. James Mallon, and guests talking about the importance of grandparents in the lives of their children and grandchildren. The four-disc series can be ordered through the EWTN religious catalogue at www .ewtnreligiouscatalogue.com, or through www.amazon.com.

• **Grandparent Camp**

This three-day grandparent camp is offered at St. Robert of Newminster Parish in Ada, Michigan. It welcomes grandparents with grandchildren ages eight to twelve. The camp features fun, food, and faith-filled activities. For additional information on the camp, contact

St. Robert of Newminster Parish
6477 Ada Dr. SE
Ada, MI 49301
Phone: 616-676-9111
E-mail: parishmail@strobertchurch.org

May God bless you. May God give you strength. May God inspire you to keep moving forward. Let us care for the family. Let us defend the family, because there our future is at stake.
—Pope Francis, Address, September 26, 2015

Questions for Reflection

1. Do you feel the need for support in your vocation as a grandparent? If so, in what ways?

2. Where have you found support? If there are no support groups in your area, how could you start one?

3. Have you reached out to other grandparents in your parish or neighborhood? What are some questions you could have ready to help spark a conversation with other grandparents?

Grandparent Prayer

Gracious and loving God, thank you for the gift of my family. Help me become a good grandparent. Help me find the support and encouragement that I need. Allow me to be a source of support and encouragement for other grandparents. Amen.

Fun and Faith with Grandchildren during Advent

Advent encompasses the first four weeks of the new liturgical year and marks the time of preparation for the celebration of the birth of Jesus. The word *Advent* stems from the Latin word *adventus*, which means "coming." Here are some fun Advent activities to share with your grandchildren as you await the coming of the Christ Child:

Make an Advent Wreath

You'll need four candleholders, three purple candles, one pink candle, and real or artificial evergreen branches to circle the candles in the shape of a wreath. Some families like to add a white Christ candle in the center, which they light on Christmas Eve.

Explain to your grandchildren that Catholics light the Advent wreath as part of their spiritual preparation for Christmas. The evergreen branches shaped into a circle represent everlasting life promised to us by Jesus. The lit candles remind us that Jesus came into the world to dispel darkness and radiate the light of God's love.

Here is a simple candle-lighting ceremony that you can use during Advent with your grandchildren:

First Week of Advent: Light the same purple candle each day and pray, *Dear God, help each person in our family to wait* *patiently for the coming of Jesus. Fill us with hope. Give us your love. Amen.*

Second Week of Advent: Light the same two purple candles each day and pray, *Dear God, help each person in our family get ready to welcome Jesus at Christmas. Open our hearts. Fill us with love. Amen.*

Third Week of Advent: Light the same two purple candles along with the pink candle each day, and pray, *Dear God, help each person in our family understand the true meaning of Christmas. Fill us with joy. Make us more loving. Amen.*

Fourth Week of Advent: Light all the candles each day and pray, *Dear God, help each person in our family experience the love of the Christ Child. Fill us with wonder and awe. Make us instruments of your love. Amen.*

Make an Advent Chain

An Advent chain will help your grandchildren count the days until Christmas. Making a chain is fun. Let the children help you cut one strip of purple construction paper for each day of Advent. Use a pink strip for the third Sunday of Advent and a white strip for Christmas. Some families like to write something special on each strip, such as *"Do something nice for someone," "Say a Hail Mary for someone who is sick,"* or *"Read a book about a saint."* Your grandchildren can brainstorm other things to write.

Use paste or tape to loop the strips into a chain. Let your grandchildren take the chain home. They can detach one link every day and read the message as they wait for Christmas.

Quiz Your Grandkids

1. How many Sundays are there in Advent?
2. What holy day of obligation falls during Advent?
3. What traditional Advent hymn expresses our longing for the coming of Jesus?
4. What color is used in church during Advent?
5. What color is used on the third Sunday of Advent?

Answers: (1) There are four Sundays in Advent. (2) The feast of the Immaculate Conception (December 8) is a holy day of obligation. (3) "O Come, O Come, Emmanuel" is a traditional Advent hymn. (4) Advent vestments and altar cloths are bluish purple, the color of royalty. (5) Pink vestments and altar cloths on the third Sunday of Advent symbolize rejoicing that we have reached the midpoint on our journey toward Christmas.

Celebrate Saints during Advent

• **Celebrate the feast of St. Nicholas on December 6.** St. Nicholas was a third-century bishop who was known as a miracle worker and a giver of secret gifts. In some homes, children put their shoes by the door or near the fireplace on the night before the feast of St. Nicholas. They wake the next morning to find candy and small trinkets left by the great saint.

- **Celebrate the feast of the Immaculate Conception on December 8.** This holy day of obligation honors Our Lady conceived without sin. If you can attend Mass with your grandchildren for this special feast day, that's great. If not, ask your grandchildren if they will pray a Hail Mary with you in person or on the telephone to mark the occasion.

- **Celebrate the feast of Our Lady of Guadalupe on December 12.** This day commemorates the appearance of Our Lady to a Mexican peasant named Juan Diego. When no one believed his story, Our Lady instructed him to go to a nearby hilltop, where he would find roses in bloom, even though it was December. It's a great day to have a Mexican dinner with your grandchildren. Or read the story of Juan Diego to them in person or on the phone. Or take your grandchildren to buy a bouquet of roses, arrange the roses in a vase, and place them at Our Lady's altar in your parish.

- **Celebrate the feast of St. Lucy on December 13.** St. Lucy was a fourth-century martyr whose name and feast day are associated with light. In Scandinavian countries, children light candles and eat special pastries. In Italy, St. Lucy brings small gifts to good children. In Hungary, children plant wheat seeds in a little pot and watch the wheat grow until Christmas Eve, when they use the wheat to soften the manger in their family's Christmas crèche. Another fun activity is making a St. Lucy's crown, which consists of braided sweet bread shaped into a crown and topped with frosting, cherries, candies, and candles.

Set Up an Interactive Nativity Scene

Start with an empty stable. Place the figures of Mary and Joseph on the other side of the room, and let your grandchildren move them closer to the crèche each day. On Christmas Eve, add Baby Jesus, the angels, and the shepherds. Then let the wise men begin their journey to the crèche so they arrive on the feast of the Epiphany.

Make a Jesse Tree

A Jesse Tree is a small artificial tree with homemade decorations that represent important people, places, and events from Jesus' family history. The tree gets its name from the prophet Isaiah, who wrote, "There shall come forth a shoot from the stump of Jesse, / and a branch shall grow out of his roots" (Isaiah 11:1.)

Jesse was the father of King David, from whom Jesus was descended. Ask your grandchildren to help make symbols to hang on the tree. Here are a few examples:

* A picture of the world, to symbolize God's creation (Genesis 1)
* Noah's ark (Genesis 6–9)
* A ram, symbolizing Abraham's sacrifice (Genesis 22:1-18)
* A coat of many colors, symbolizing Joseph and his brothers (Genesis 37)
* Stone tablets, representing the Ten Commandments (Exodus 20:1-17)
* A crown, representing King David (2 Samuel 5:1-5)
* Flowing water to represent John the Baptist (Mark 1:1-8)

- A picture of Our Lady (Luke 1:26-38)
- A hammer, representing St. Joseph, the carpenter (Matthew 1:18-25)
- The star that appeared over the stable in Bethlehem (Matthew 2:1-10)
- A picture of Baby Jesus in the manger (Luke 2:1-20)

Help Other People

Here are some ways your grandchildren can join you in reaching out to others during Advent:

- Ask them to help you buy and wrap a Christmas gift for a needy child.
- Shop for nonperishable food that you can bring to a food pantry.
- Visit a friend or relative in a nursing home.
- Bake Christmas cookies for a homebound neighbor.

> In this season of Advent, let us be guided by the Baptist's exhortation: "Prepare the way of the Lord, make his paths straight!" (Matthew 3:3).
> —Pope Francis, Angelus, December 4, 2016

Fun and Faith with Grandchildren during the Christmas Season

The Christmas season begins with vigil Masses on Christmas Eve and ends with the feast of the Baptism of the Lord. This special time, when your grandchildren are off from school for Christmas vacation, offers a great opportunity for Christmas fun and faith. Here are some ideas:

Celebrate the Twelve Days of Christmas

Secular society typically wraps up the Christmas season on January 1. But traditionally, Christmas Day is considered the first day of Christmas, and the celebrations continue for the next twelve days through January 5. You can reclaim this tradition by doing something special with your grandchildren on each of the twelve days. It might be something as simple as singing "The Twelve Days of Christmas" in person or on the phone. You could give your grandchildren stickers or toy trinkets each day. Or you could relate the twelve days to the twelve months in the coming year and plan a special project or event for each month. Part of the fun will be deciding together what you want to do to celebrate.

Read the Christmas Story

Read the Gospel accounts of the birth of Jesus to your grand-children. You can find them in the Bible: Matthew 1:18-23 and Luke 2:1-20. With little ones, you might want to paraphrase the story or read from a children's Bible.

Sing Christmas Carols

Teach your grandchildren traditional Christmas carols that celebrate the birth of Jesus. It might be fun to invite them for an evening of caroling.

Stage Your Own Christmas Pageant

Get your grandchildren together and let them act out the Christmas story in your living room. Older grandchildren can help with costumes and props. Here is a simple script that includes narration and Christmas carols:

Narrator: Welcome to our Christmas pageant. Christmas is a very special time for children. This year our special gift to you is a journey back in time to the very first Christmas, when God gave us the best gift of all. It started with a young woman named Mary who was engaged to a man named Joseph. One day an angel came to Mary and said:

Angel: The Lord is with you, Mary. Blessed are you among women.

Narrator: Mary was deeply troubled by his words and worried about what his greeting meant. But the angel went on to say:

Angel: Do not be afraid. You have found favor with God. You will have a son and give him the name Jesus.

Narrator: Mary wondered how this could happen. But the angel told her that the Holy Spirit would come upon her, and the baby would be called the Son of God. Mary replied:

Mary: I am the servant of the Lord. Let it be done to me as you say.

Narrator: And so it came to pass that Caesar Augustus published a decree ordering a census of the whole world. Everyone went to register in his own town. Joseph went with Mary to the town of Bethlehem to register.

Song: "O Little Town of Bethlehem"

Narrator: When they reached Bethlehem after a long and tiring journey, they began to look for a place to stay.

Joseph to Innkeeper: Do you have any rooms?

Innkeeper: No. But we have a stable where you can stay.

Narrator: While they were in the stable, the time arrived for Mary's child to be born. She gave birth to a son, and she wrapped him in swaddling clothes and laid him in a manger.

Song: "Away in a Manger"

Narrator: In the countryside close by were shepherds, who lived in the fields and took turns watching their flocks by night. Suddenly the angel of the Lord appeared to them, and they were afraid. But the angel said:

Angel: Fear not. For I bring you good tidings of great joy, which will be shared by all people. For unto you this day in the city of David is born a Savior, who is Christ the Lord. And this shall be a sign to you: you will find the baby wrapped in swaddling clothes and lying in a manger.

Narrator: And suddenly there appeared with the angel a multitude of angels praising God and singing:

Song: "Joy to the World"

Narrator: And the shepherds said to one another:

Shepherd: Let us go into Bethlehem and see this baby.

Song: "Angels We Have Heard on High"

Narrator: And the shepherds found Mary and Joseph and the baby in the stable, just as the angel had said.

Song: "Silent Night"

Narrator: And in the east, some wise men saw a star and said:

Wise Man: Where is this baby? We saw his star when it came up in the east, and we want to worship him.

Song: "We Three Kings"

Narrator: The wise men followed the star until it stopped over the place where Jesus was. When they saw Jesus with Mary, they knelt down and worshipped him. They brought gifts of gold, frankincense, and myrrh.

Narrator: Jesus was in the world, and through him the world was made, yet the world did not know who he was. And anyone who did accept him, he empowered to become a child of God.

Song: "O Come, All Ye Faithful"

Narrator: From all of us to all of you, Merry Christmas!

Song: "We Wish You a Merry Christmas"

Quiz Your Grandkids

1. What color is used in church during the Christmas season?
2. Why was Jesus born in a stable?
3. How many wise men came to visit Jesus?
4. Where did Mary and Joseph take Jesus after they left Bethlehem?
5. Whose feast day do we celebrate on the day after Christmas?

Answers: (1) The color white is used for vestments and altar cloths, to symbolize the light, innocence, purity, and joy of the Christmas season. (2) Jesus was born in a stable because there was no room in the inn. (3) Three wise men came to visit Jesus. (4) Mary and Joseph took Jesus to Egypt after they left Bethlehem. (5) We celebrate the feast of St. Stephen, the first martyr, on December 26.

Share the Story of the Christmas Crèche

In 1223, St. Francis of Assisi set up the first Christmas crèche in a cave in Italy. When people from the village came to see the manger with its hay and live ox and donkey, St. Francis spoke to them about the newborn baby in Bethlehem. The idea of setting up a nativity scene spread rapidly throughout Europe. You might want to invite your grandchildren to visit the Christmas crèche in your parish church. Suggest that they pray to the Baby Jesus for their special intentions.

Ring in the New Year

Invite your grandchildren to sleep over on New Year's Eve, and have your own celebration with sparkling grape juice, noise-makers, and fun. For younger kids, turn the clock ahead so that they stay awake until the clock strikes twelve—even though it might really be eight o'clock! At "midnight," share kisses, hugs, and special wishes for the coming year.

Go to Mass on New Year's Day

Don't forget that New Year's Day is a holy day of obligation. What better way to start the New Year than going to Mass with your grandchildren, followed by a delicious brunch?

Follow the Christmas Star

On January 6, we celebrate the visit of the three wise men to the Baby Jesus. The feast is called the Epiphany, a word that means "to reveal." The wise men experienced the presence of God that day and bowed down to worship him with gifts of gold, frankincense, and myrrh.

Share with your grandchildren the different ways that God has revealed himself to you in people, places, and things.

- Maybe it happened in your childhood, when you were at prayer or receiving the Eucharist.

- Maybe it happened during a painful time, when you realized that you were not alone and that the Lord was there to comfort and support you.

- Maybe it happened at a time of indecision, when you suddenly felt that God was leading you in a specific direction.

- Maybe it happened when you found yourself in a state of awe over the beauty of nature or the wonder of creation.

- Maybe it happened when you were filled with joy at your marriage, the births of your children, the births of your grandchildren, or some other moment when you knew that God was present in your life.

Sharing these "God moments" with your grandchildren is one of the best ways to pass along your Catholic faith.

With the shepherds, let us enter into the real Christmas, bringing to Jesus all that we are, our alienation, our unhealed wounds, our sins. Then, in Jesus, we will enjoy the taste of the true spirit of Christmas: the beauty of being loved by God. With Mary and Joseph, let us pause before the manger, before Jesus who is born as bread for my life. Contemplating his humble and infinite love, let us simply tell him: Thank you. Thank you because you have done all this *for me*.

—Pope Francis, Homily, December 24, 2016

—Appendix C—

Fun and Faith with Grandchildren during Lent

Lent is a time for self-sacrifice, repentance, and conversion of heart. It is also a great time to help your grandchildren experience some of the most thought-provoking and powerful traditions in our Catholic faith. Here are some suggestions:

Ashes

Ash Wednesday, the official beginning of Lent, is the day you can bring your grandchildren to church to receive ashes. If you can't bring them, you can explain to them why they will see people walking around with smudges on their foreheads. Tell them that marking a person's forehead is an ancient symbol of ownership. Receiving ashes in the shape of a cross on your forehead identifies a person as a disciple of Jesus Christ. The ashes also serve as reminders of human mortality and the need for repentance.

Tell the Story of Pretzels

Share the story of how pretzels originated in Europe during the Middle Ages. A monk was making unleavened bread for Lent with flour and water because eggs, milk, and lard were not consumed in the Lenten fast. The monk twisted some dough into the shape of people praying with both arms folded across their chests. He called them *pretiola*, the Latin word meaning "little reward," and he gave them to children who were learning to say their prayers. You can make the story even more fun by making your own pretzels.

Quiz Your Grandkids

1. How many days are there in Lent?
2. What color is used in parishes during Lent?
3. What prayers are omitted from Mass during Lent?
4. What does the word *Lent* mean?
5. How many days do Catholics fast during Lent?

Answers: (1) There are forty days in Lent. (2) The Lenten liturgical color is purple, the color of royalty, which symbolizes the suffering of Jesus our King and anticipates the glory of the resurrection. (3) During Lent the Gloria and the word *alleluia* are omitted from the Mass. (4) The word *Lent* comes from an Anglo-Saxon word that means "lengthen," a reference to lengthening days as spring approaches. (5) Two, Ash Wednesday and Good Friday. Catholics also abstain from meat on those days plus the five Fridays during Lent.

Celebrate Saint Days during Lent

- **March 17** is the feast of St. Patrick, who dedicated his life to converting the Irish people to Catholicism. Celebrate by reading the story of St. Patrick, who was abducted by pirates from his home in Britain, enslaved in Ireland, escaped back to Britain, and eventually returned to Ireland in response to a dream in which he heard the Irish people asking "the holy servant boy" to "return and walk among us." St. Patrick is well-known for his use of a shamrock to explain the mystery of the Blessed Trinity—one God in three Persons. You might want to wear green and sample special Irish foods. Some communities celebrate with a parade.

- **March 19** is the feast of St. Joseph, who is honored as the husband of Our Lady and the foster father of Jesus. Celebrate by bringing your grandchildren to a St. Joseph Table. According to tradition, this custom started in Sicily after the people prayed to St. Joseph to intercede for the end of a devastating famine. When their prayers were answered, they cooked a meatless meal because it was Lent and invited everyone in the village to celebrate in thanksgiving to God.

   Today many parishes host a St. Joseph Table, or you can have your own festive dinner at home. Look online to find ideas for foods that have special symbolism for the St. Joseph's Table.

Do unto Others

Almsgiving and service to the poor and the sick have always been important parts of Lent. Here are some ideas for teaching your grandchildren to care about those who are less fortunate:

- Take your grandchildren grocery shopping, and bring the food to the St. Vincent de Paul Society or to your local food bank.

- Let your grandchildren light a candle at church for people who are sick or suffering.

- Ask your grandchildren to help you clean out closets. Donate gently used items.

- Explore various Catholic missions online, and let your grandchildren pick a mission and send money, clothing, or supplies.

- Volunteer with your grandchildren to help with a service project in your parish. Whether it's working in the parish gardens, cleaning the church, changing the missalettes in the pews, or assisting with the parish food or clothing drive, it is a chance to serve together.

- Encourage your grandchildren to do something nice for someone every day during Lent.

Some Questions Your Grandkids Might Ask about Lent

1. Why do the dates of Ash Wednesday and Easter change?
Easter is celebrated on the first Sunday after the first full moon following the spring equinox. It can occur as early as March 22 or as late as April 25. Ash Wednesday is forty-six days before Easter Sunday.

2. Where do they get the ashes?
Palm branches from the previous Palm Sunday are burned. The ashes are blessed, sprinkled with holy water, and incensed.

3. How long should we leave the ashes on our foreheads?
They should remain all day. Wash them off before going to bed.

4. Why do some parishes put sand in the holy water fonts during Lent? Sand is a reminder that Lent is a "desert experience" during which we thirst for the baptismal water of Easter.

5. Why does the priest wear pink during Lent?
Rose-colored vestments and a more joyful tone are used on Laetare Sunday, the halfway point in the Lenten season, as we anticipate the coming of Easter.

Lenten Prayers and Devotions

- Say an Our Father on the phone or in person with your grandchildren every day during Lent.

- Attend Mass together whenever possible.

- Pray the sorrowful mysteries of the Rosary with your grandchildren.

- Invite your grandchildren to your parish penance service.

- Start a family journal with spiritual insights, the names of people who need prayers, a list of hurts or disappointments to offer up, and special intentions.

- Teach your grandchildren how to pray the Stations of the Cross.

Stations of the Cross

Explain to your grandchildren that remembering the suffering, death, and resurrection of Jesus was important for the early Christians. By the late fourth century, people made pilgrimages to the Holy Land and followed the path Jesus took to Calvary. During the Middle Ages, when wars made it impossible to travel, people created a *Via Dolorosa*, or "Sorrowful Way" in their town or village. They erected paintings or sculptures depicting the passion of Christ along a processional route or inside a church. By the mid-eighteenth century, the number of stations was fixed at fourteen, and the devotion known as the Stations of the Cross became widespread.

> Let us not waste this season of Lent, so favorable a time for conversion! We ask this through the maternal intercession of the Virgin Mary, who, encountering the greatness of God's mercy freely bestowed upon her, was the first to acknowledge her lowliness (cf. Luke 1:48) and to call herself the Lord's humble servant (cf. 1:38).
> —Pope Francis, Message for Lent, October 4, 2015

Fun and Faith with Grandchildren during Holy Week

Holy Week starts on Palm Sunday and ends at sundown on Holy Saturday. In addition to being a week of preparation for the great feast of Easter, it is also the most solemn time in the Church year. Here are some practical ways to help make Holy Week both meaningful and fun for the whole family:

Share the Story

Find age-appropriate books that tell the story of Holy Week. Then attend Holy Week liturgies in your parish, and help your grandchildren make the liturgical connection to the stories during the blessing of the palms, the washing of the feet, and the Good Friday liturgy.

Help Your Grandchildren Understand the Cross

Explain that Jesus died on a cross, but three days later on Easter Sunday, God brought him back to life. That's how we know that the cross always leads to something good.

Acknowledge that everybody has difficulties in life. Sometimes we say our problems are the crosses that we carry. Like Jesus, we don't want problems, but we know that God will help us when bad things happen.

Find an example in your own life of a cross that you or a family member had to bear, and share how something good came from it. Talk about some of the crosses your grandchildren might experience in their lives. Encourage your grandchildren to pray that Jesus will help them with their crosses.

Some Questions Your Grandkids Might Ask about Holy Week

- **Why do we use the word *passion* to describe the suffering of Jesus?**

The word *passion* comes from a Latin word for suffering. When referring to the events leading up to the death of Jesus, people sometimes capitalize the word *passion* to differentiate it from the modern meaning of the word.

- **Why do some parishes cover crosses, crucifixes, and statues during Holy Week?**

Before 1970, it was customary to cover crosses, crucifixes, and statues during the last two weeks of Lent. After 1970, the practice was left to the discretion of each diocese. In 1995, the United States Bishops' Committee on the Liturgy gave individual parishes permission to reinstate the practice on their own. The veiling helps to remind us that without the cross and resurrection, we could not be saved, and it also heightens our sense of anticipation of Easter.

- **Why do we call it Good Friday?**

In the English language, the term *Good Friday* probably evolved from "God's Friday," in the same way that *good-bye* evolved from "God be with you."

- **Who decided the date of Easter?**

In 325, the Council of Nicaea decreed that Easter would be celebrated on the Sunday following the first full moon after the spring equinox.

Make Holy Week Eggs

Fill plastic eggs with items that reflect the events of Holy Week.

- **On Palm Sunday,** give your grandchildren plastic eggs that contain a piece of palm, a furry fabric that represents the donkey Jesus rode, and a picture of Jesus smiling.

- **On Holy Thursday,** they might find a piece of towel recalling the washing of feet, a cracker symbolizing the Last Supper, three dimes to recall the thirty pieces of silver, and a picture of a rooster to remind them of Peter's denial.

- **On Good Friday,** the eggs might contain a crucifix, dice to recall the casting of lots for Jesus' clothes, and a picture of Jesus looking sad.

Quiz Your Grandkids

1. Where did Jesus' agony take place?
2. Who betrayed Jesus?
3. Who denied Jesus three times?
4. Who ordered Jesus to be scourged?
5. What criminal was released instead of Jesus?
6. How many Stations of the Cross are there?
7. How many times did Jesus fall on the way to Calvary?
8. Who helped Jesus carry his cross?
9. Who wiped the face of Jesus?
10. Who arranged for the burial of Jesus?

Answers: (1) The agony took place in the Garden of Gethsemane, which is on the Mount of Olives. (2) Judas betrayed Jesus. (3) Peter denied Jesus. (4) Pontius Pilate ordered Jesus to be scourged. (5) The crowd demanded the release of Barabbas instead of Jesus. (6) There are fourteen stations. (7) Jesus fell three times. (8) Simon of Cyrene helped Jesus carry his cross. (9) Veronica wiped the face of Jesus. (10) Joseph of Arimathea arranged for the burial of Jesus.

Other Ideas for Holy Week

- Teach your grandchildren how to make crosses out of the blessed palms.

- Combine a secular tradition with the sacred. Before coloring Easter eggs, let your grandchildren write messages on the eggs in crayon that celebrate the true meaning of Easter.

For example, "Christ is Risen," "Alleluia," or "Jesus loves us."

- On Holy Thursday, emphasize the importance of serving others by helping someone in need.

- Acknowledge the sadness of Good Friday by encouraging your grandchildren to write letters or draw pictures for family members or friends who are grieving the loss of loved ones.

- If your parish is having a blessing of Easter foods on Holy Saturday, let your grandchildren pack a basket with butter, eggs, sweet breads, and other items that your family will enjoy on Easter Sunday.

> I remember, excuse me, a personal story. As a child, every Good Friday my grandmother took us to the Procession of Candles, and at the end of the procession came the recumbent Christ, and my grandmother made us kneel down. She told us, 'Children, look, he is dead, but tomorrow he will be risen!' That is how the faith entered: faith in Christ Crucified and Risen.
>
> —Pope Francis, Homily, May 3, 2013

—*Appendix E*—

Fun and Faith with Grandchildren during the Easter Season

The Easter Season begins at the Easter Vigil and lasts for the next fifty days, culminating on Pentecost Sunday, when we remember how the Holy Spirit descended on the disciples who were gathered in the upper room. These fifty days offer great opportunities for grandparents to share faith and fun with their grandchildren.

Share the Story

Read to your grandchildren the Scripture passages that describe the resurrection of Jesus. For younger grandchildren, you might want to paraphrase or read from a children's Bible. Here are the Gospel citations: Matthew 28:1-10; Mark 16:1-8; Luke 24:13-35; John 20:1-9.

Explain to your grandchildren that the death and resurrection of Jesus is a great paradox. What seemed to be over was just the beginning. What seemed to be a terrible tragedy was transformed into the greatest miracle of all time.

Keep Christ in Easter

How can you and your grandchildren celebrate the real meaning of Christ's glorious resurrection in the midst of bunnies, eggs, hams, and lambs? Start by explaining that these seemingly secular Easter traditions were once meaningful ways to celebrate the good news that Jesus rose from the dead. They simply lost their true meaning over the years. But it's not too late to bring the symbolism back to life. Here are some suggestions to help you explain to your grandchildren the spiritual foundations for many of the secular symbols and activities of the Easter season:

- **Colored Eggs:** Eggs were a pagan symbol of rebirth at springtime. Christians adopted the egg as a symbol of the new life that comes with the resurrection. Dying eggs in bright colors became popular during the Middle Ages. The colored eggs were a special treat on Easter morning, because most people refrained from eating meat and eggs as part of their Lenten fast.

- **Spring Housecleaning:** In many cultures, the Monday, Tuesday, and Wednesday of Holy Week are designated as days for vigorous housecleaning in preparation for Easter. This custom probably evolved from the Jewish custom of ritual cleaning before Passover.

- **Easter Lilies:** Using white lilies as Easter decorations in homes and churches came into practice in the 1800s. The white flower is a symbol of purity. The lily's trumpetlike shape heralds the triumph of Jesus over death.

- **Easter Baskets:** The tradition began in Eastern Europe. People brought their food for Easter Sunday to church in a basket on Holy Saturday, to receive a special blessing. The tradition of blessing Easter food continues in many parishes today.

- **The Easter Bunny:** The Pennsylvania Dutch introduced the tradition of an *Oschter Haws*, or Easter Hare, who brought colored eggs to good children on Easter morning. Like the decorated eggs, the bunny was a symbol of new life in Christ.

- **Jelly Beans:** These popular candies were invented in the 1800s, but they didn't become part of the Easter tradition until the 1930s. Because they were egg shaped, they were also thought to symbolize new life and spiritual rebirth.

- **Lamb:** The Jews sacrificed a lamb at Passover, and Scripture refers to Jesus as the Lamb of God, sacrificed for us, the one who takes away the sins of the world. Lamb is a traditional Easter dish. In some Eastern European countries, butter is molded into the shape of a lamb for Easter Sunday breakfast and dinner.

- **Ham:** Ham became an Easter favorite for a very practical (rather than spiritual) reason. In the days before refrigeration, pigs were butchered in the fall, and their meat was cured during the winter months. The first hams, which had undergone the transformation from fresh pork, were ready at Easter time, making ham the perfect choice for an Easter celebration.

- **Sweet Breads:** In pagan times, people made wheat cakes and offered them to the goddess of spring. Christians adopted the tradition by baking special sweet breads, cakes, and pastries as a special treat to celebrate Easter and the end of the long Lenten fast.

- **Easter Clothes:** The custom of wearing new clothes on Easter originated from the early Christians, who clothed the newly baptized in white garments at the Easter vigil to represent their new life in Christ.

Invite Your Grandchildren to Be "Easter People"

On Easter Sunday, we celebrate the resurrection of Jesus. The word *resurrection* refers to "standing up again." Jesus "stood up again" on Easter, when he emerged from the tomb. As Easter people, we can stand up against evil. We can stand up when something bad happens in our lives. We can stand up and admit when we have done something wrong.

During the Easter season, we have a chance to focus on what resurrection means in our lives. Younger grandchildren probably won't understand the concept. But you can ask your tween and teen grandchildren how they will live as Easter people who stand up for what is right.

- Can they stand up for something that is important at school, in sports, or in the community?
- Can they say no to something that is wrong?
- Can they let go of bad habits, judgmental attitudes, and negative outlooks?
- Can they let go of anger and resentment toward people who hurt them?
- Can they ask for forgiveness from someone they have hurt?

- Can they reach out to someone who needs a kind word or a helping hand?
- Can they cultivate a sense of gratitude to God for all the good things in their lives?

Celebrate Divine Mercy Sunday

On the first Sunday after Easter, we celebrate God's mercy, which is greater than any sin we may ever commit. This special feast day, commonly known as Divine Mercy Sunday, was established by Pope John Paul II on April 30, 2000, and now is observed by Catholics all over the world. The liturgical readings for Divine Mercy Sunday focus on God's mercy and the forgiveness of sins.

The inspiration for Divine Mercy Sunday can be found in the diary of St. Faustina Kowalska, a Polish nun who experienced apparitions of Jesus and recorded his messages. In 1935, Sr. Faustina reported a vision that gave birth to the Chaplet of Divine Mercy, a series of prayers that are recited on rosary beads. In several other apparitions, Jesus asked for prayer and meditation every afternoon at three o'clock in remembrance of his death on the cross.

Here are step-by-step instructions for teaching your grandchildren how to pray the Divine Mercy Chaplet on the rosary beads:

1. Make the Sign of the Cross with the crucifix.
2. On the first bead, repeat three times: "O blood and water, which gushed forth from the heart of Jesus as a fountain of mercy for us, I trust in you!"

3. On the next three beads, pray the Our Father, the Hail Mary, and the Apostles' Creed.

4. On the fifth bead, pray; "Eternal Father, I offer you the Body and Blood, Soul and Divinity of your dearly beloved Son, Our Lord, Jesus Christ, in atonement for our sins and those of the whole world."

5. On each of the first set of ten beads, pray, "For the sake of his sorrowful Passion, have mercy on us and on the whole world."

6. Repeat for the remaining decades, praying the "Eternal Father" prayer on the Our Father bead and the "For the sake of his sorrowful Passion" prayer on each of the Hail Mary beads.

7. Conclude by praying three times: "Holy God, Holy Mighty One, Holy Immortal One, have mercy on us and on the whole world."

Quiz Your Grandkids

1. Who was the first person to discover that Jesus had risen from the dead?

2. What does the Easter candle symbolize?

3. What color vestments does the priest wear during the Easter season?

4. What word is said and sung frequently throughout the Easter season?

5. What promises do we renew during the Easter season?

Answers: (1) Mary Magdalene was the first to arrive at the empty tomb. (2) The Easter candle is a symbol of the light of

Christ, a powerful reminder that Jesus is light in the darkness. (3) The priest's vestments and the altar cloths are white. (4) The word *alleluia*, which means "God be praised," is said and sung frequently throughout the Easter season. (5) We renew our baptismal promises during the Easter vigil and on Easter Sunday.

Read the Acts of the Apostles

The Acts of the Apostles tells the story of the early Christians after the death and resurrection of Jesus. It's an amazing story, with lots of drama, miracles, and even some disagreements. It's a story that might provoke some interesting discussions with your tween and teen grandchildren.

Celebrate the Ascension of Jesus into Heaven

Read the story about how Jesus led the disciples out of town, blessed them, and then rose into heaven (Luke 24:50-51; Acts 1:8-9). Then let your grandchildren release helium balloons to mark the occasion. You can also encourage your grandchildren to draw a picture of the ascension and other events that took place during the Easter season.

Take a New-Life Walk

Spring is a time of new promise, new life, and new energy. We feel ourselves being restored, renewed, and recreated. One way to reinforce the Easter season in the minds of your grandchildren is to take a new-life walk. It's a perfect opportunity to help your grandchildren appreciate the magnificence of God's creation. Here are some things you might experience:

- **Spring Showers:** Get out your rain gear and splash through puddles. This offers a wonderful opportunity to talk to your grandkids about God's gift of rain. Most people don't realize that there is a limited amount of water in the world, and this water keeps recycling itself in what is called the "water cycle." Explain that the puddles they splash through today will eventually dry up, but the water doesn't disappear. It goes into the air in the form of vapor. When the air gets cold, the water vapor in the air forms clouds. When the clouds get too full of water, it rains. As the rain falls, the water creates new puddles—puddles you can again splash through—and you're back to the beginning of the water cycle.

- **Budding Trees:** Look for buds on the trees. Explain to your grandchildren that the buds formed last summer but stopped growing during the fall and winter. The warm spring sunshine wakes up the buds, and they begin to grow. You will begin to see tiny shoots sprouting, and before long the branches will be thick with leaves. This is a great time to talk to your grandchildren about the miracle of growth.

- **Babbling Brooks:** Watching the springtime rush of water in a creek or stream is great fun. Tell your grandchildren how melting snow and springtime rain make the streams swell and dance over the rocks. Early in the spring, you may notice pieces of ice floating in the water. Later in the spring, you may see tadpoles in the water. It's a wonderful opportunity to explain to your grandkids that God's gift of water is essential for sustaining life.

- **Wind:** Take a walk in the wind. Sometimes wind blows so softly that you only know air is moving because you see a flag flicker or hear a leaf rustle. But at other times, wind rocks the branches of the trees and blows things all over the place. If you're walking into a strong wind, it's a real effort. If you're walking with a strong wind, you can feel it blow you along. You can explain that we experience God in the same way that we feel the wind—we can't see God, but we can feel God's presence.

- **Beautiful Blooms:** As you stroll around the neighborhood, identify the different shapes, sizes, and colors of springtime flowers. Crocuses are usually the first to blossom, and later you'll want to look for tulips, daffodils, and flowering bushes like azaleas and rhododendrons. It's also fun to hike through a field and gather wild flowers. This is an opportunity to talk to your grandkids about the beauty of God's creation.

- **Blossoming Fruit Trees:** Plan a springtime trip to an orchard to see fruit trees in bloom. Let your grandchildren smell the fragrance of the blossoms. Explain how the petals from the pink and white blossoms will fall off and how apples, peaches, pears, and cherries will begin to form. Plan to bring your grandchildren back in the summer and fall, when the fresh fruit is being harvested. It's a great opportunity to help your grandkids understand how God created fruits and vegetables for people to eat.

- **New Baby Animals:** Be on the lookout for baby animals that are born in the spring. A mother duck will lay between five and twelve eggs and sit on her nest until they hatch. A mother squirrel builds her nest in a tree, and she usually has between two and five babies in the nest with her, until they are about six weeks old. Bunnies are also born in a nest, which the mother burrows into a bed of fur in the ground, coming back to the nest only once a day to feed them. Baby birds stay in their nests until they learn to fly. The mother or father bird will bring them worms and insects to eat. This is a perfect time to explain to your grandchildren that God cares for us in the same way that parents care for their babies.

- **Bird-Watching:** Spring is a wonderful time to introduce your grandchildren to bird-watching. You can get started right in your own backyard. All you need is a beginner's guide to help you identify different types of birds that are common in your part of the country.

  With little kids, you can just point to different birds and notice differences in size or color. Older grandchildren might appreciate their own binoculars. The binoculars don't have to be expensive, and it's fun when everyone can look closely at a bird at the same time. Bird-watching gives you the opportunity to help your grandchildren appreciate the beauty and the diversity of God's creation.

During this Easter season, when the Church invites us to give thanks for God's mercy and the new life we have received from the risen Christ, I pray that you will experience the joy born of gratitude for the Lord's many gifts, and seek to serve him in the least of his brothers and sisters.
—Pope Francis, Address, April 11, 2013

Fun and Faith with Grandchildren during Pentecost

What are you doing for Pentecost this year? It's a question that you probably don't hear much. In fact, many people don't really understand what Pentecost is or why it is so important in the Church calendar.

Pentecost Sunday is the birthday of the Church. It marks the day when the fearful apostles, who had gathered in an upper room after Jesus ascended into heaven, were suddenly filled with the Holy Spirit and went boldly into the streets to tell everyone about Jesus. Each person in the crowd, even though they were from different countries and spoke different languages, understood the apostles in their own language. Thousands became believers that day.

Here are some suggestions on how to make Pentecost a special day for you and your grandchildren:

Celebrate the Birthday of the Church

- Make a birthday cake, and sing "Happy Birthday" to the Church.
- Say a special prayer for the Church.
- Read the account of Pentecost in the Acts of the Apostles (Acts 2).
- Remind your grandchildren that they received the Holy Spirit at their baptism.

- Dress in red, the color of fire and a symbol of the Holy Spirit.
- Decorate with paper doves, which are symbols of the Holy Spirit.
- Ask your grandchildren to help you look on the Internet for a Catholic mission that spreads the good news of Jesus to others. Make a donation to the mission as a birthday gift to the Church.

Talk about the Holy Spirit with Your Grandchildren

The Holy Spirit is the Third Person of the Blessed Trinity—one God in three Persons, Father, Son, and Holy Spirit. The Trinity is one of the most profound mysteries of our faith. Some people explain the Holy Spirit as the power of love and truth that emanates from the Father and the Son.

Read the references to the Holy Spirit in the Bible, particularly in the Gospel of John and the Acts of the Apostles, and discuss them with your grandchildren. Explain to your grandchildren that whenever you feel as if you are being called by God or inspired to do something good, it is the work of the Holy Spirit.

One of the most important lessons you can teach your grandchildren is how to listen to the Holy Spirit. Ask them if they have any ideas about how they can call upon the Holy Spirit to lead and guide them. Begin by asking your grandchildren after Mass what they heard in the readings, in the music, in the homily, or in their prayers after Communion. Then help them recognize that these are ways the Holy Spirit works in their lives.

The Gifts of the Holy Spirit

The spiritual gifts that the Holy Spirit brings are wisdom, understanding, knowledge, good judgment, courage, reverence, and awe (see Isaiah 11:2). As a fun Pentecost activity, write each gift on a small piece of paper, and put the papers in a basket. Let family members choose a gift. Talk about what that gift means in their lives and how they can use that gift.

The Fruits of the Holy Sprit

The fruits of the Holy Spirit are "love, joy, peace, patience, kindness, goodness, faithfulness, gentleness, self-control" (Galatians 5:22-23). Explain to your grandchildren that when we recognize the fruits of the Holy Spirit in our own lives or in the lives of other people, we can trust that the Holy Spirit is present. Talk about times when you recognized the presence of the Holy Spirit in your life. Ask them about times when they recognized the presence of the Holy Spirit in their lives.

A fundamental element of Pentecost is *astonishment*. Our God is a God of *astonishment*, this we know. No one expected anything more from the disciples: after Jesus' death they were a small, insignificant group of defeated orphans of their Master. There occurred instead an unexpected event that astounded: the people were astonished because each of them heard the disciples speaking in their own tongues, telling of the great works of God (cf. Acts 2:6-7, 11). The Church born at Pentecost is an astounding community because, with the force of her arrival from God, a new message is proclaimed—the Resurrection of Christ—with a new language—the universal one of love. A new proclamation: Christ lives, he is risen; a new language: the language of love. The disciples are adorned with power from above and speak with courage—only minutes before they all were cowardly, but now they speak with courage and candor, with the freedom of the Holy Spirit.

—Pope Francis, *Regina Caeli*, June 8, 2014

Notes

1. E-mail exchange with Dr. Karl Pillemer.

2. Arthur Kornhaber, *The Grandparent Guide: The Definitive Guide to Coping with the Challenges of Modern Grandparenting*, McGraw Hill Professional, 2002.

3. Dr. Andrew Adesman, MD, presented this study at the Pediatric Academic Societies Meeting in San Francisco, May 6–9, 2017. https://www.sciencedaily.com/releases/2017/05/170504083052. htm.

4. For information on improperly installed car seats, see https://www.today.com/parents/babies-risk-most-new-parents-are-doing-car-seats-all-2D80208999.

5. KidsHealth is a website with information about health, behavior, and development of children from before birth through the teen years. It is part of the Nemours Center for Children's Health Media. The Nemours Foundation is a nonprofit organization created by Alfred I. duPont in 1936 and is devoted to improving the health of children. Information on the survey cited in this chapter can be found at http://kidshealth.org/en/kids/comments-summer. html?ref=search&WT.ac=msh-k-dtop-en-search-clk.

6. Vern L. Bengtson, "Beyond the Nuclear Family: The Increasing Importance of Multigenerational Bonds," *Journal of Marriage and Family*, February 2001. http://www.unc.edu/~ldpearce/soci820/Readings/bengston.pdf.

7. Alan Cooperman, "Many Americans don't argue about religion—or even talk about it," Pew Research Center, April

15, 2016. http://www.pewresearch.org/fact-tank/2016/04/15/many-americans-dont-argue-about-religion-or-even-talk-about-it/

8. Telephone interview with Fr. James Mallon.

9. Nicola Ross, Malcolm Hill, Helen Sweeting and Sarah Cunningham-Burley, *Grandparents and Teen Grandchildren: Exploring Intergenerational Relationships,* report of a study funded by the Centre for Research on Families and Relationships and The Economic and Social Research Council. http://silverinnings.in/wp-content/uploads/2016/10/Grandparents_Teen_Children.pdf.

10. E-mail exchange with Dr. Karl Pillemer.

11. Telephone interview with Fr. Mallon.

12. St. Augustine, *Confessions*, Book 3, Chapter 12. https://www.ling.upenn.edu/courses/hum100/augustinconf.pdf

13. Telephone interview with Fr. Mallon.

14. Julia Griggs, Jo-Pei Tan, Ann Buchanan, Shalhevet Attar-Schwartz, Eirini Flouri, "'They've Always Been There for Me': Grandparental Involvement and Child Well-Being," *Children & Society*, Volume 24, Issue 3, May 2010, pages 200–214. http://onlinelibrary.wiley.com/doi/10.1111/j.1099-0860.2009.00215.x/abstract.

15. See Adelaide Mena, "Catholics Continue to Have Lowest Divorce Rates," *National Catholic Register,* October 2, 2013, ncregister.com/daily-news/catholics-continue-to-have-lowest-divorce-rates.

the WORD
among us®
The *Spirit* of Catholic Living

This book was published by The Word Among Us. Since 1981, The Word Among Us has been answering the call of the Second Vatican Council to help Catholic laypeople encounter Christ in the Scriptures.

The name of our company comes from the prologue to the Gospel of John and reflects the vision and purpose of all of our publications: to be an instrument of the Spirit, whose desire is to manifest Jesus' presence in and to the children of God. In this way, we hope to con-tribute to the Church's ongoing mission of proclaiming the gospel to the world so that all people would know the love and mercy of our Lord and grow more deeply in their faith as missionary disciples.

Our monthly devotional magazine, *The Word Among Us*, features meditations on the daily and Sunday Mass readings, and currently reaches more than one million Catholics in North America and another half million Catholics in one hundred countries around the world. Our book division, The Word Among Us Press, publishes numerous books, Bible studies, and pamphlets that help Catholics grow in their faith.

To learn more about who we are and what we publish, visit us at www.wau.org. There you will find a variety of Catholic resources that will help you grow in your faith.

Embrace His Word, Listen to God . . .

www.wau.org

Made in the USA
Monee, IL
22 July 2022

10100526R00128